Janet Frame was born in Dunedin, New Zealand, in 1924. Her works include ten novels, among them *Owls Do Cry*, *A State of Siege*, *Scented Gardens for the Blind*, *Yellow Flowers in the Antipodean Room*, *Faces in the Water*, and *Living in the Maniototo*, which won the Fiction Prize, New Zealand Book Awards, 1980. She has also had published four collections of stories and sketches, a volume of poetry and a children's book, *Mona Minim and the Smell of the Sun*. Janet Frame has won a number of distinctions in her native country and was awarded a CBE in the 1983 Queen's Birthday Honours List. She is New Zealand's most distinguished living novelist.

To the Is-Land, the first volume of her autobiography, won the New Zealand literary prize the James Wattie Book of the Year award in 1983.

JANET FRAME

An Angel At My Table

Autobiography 2

Reste tranquille, si soudain
L'Ange à ta table se décide;
Efface doucement les quelques rides
Que fait la nappe sous ton pain

Rilke, *Vergers*

PALADIN
GRAFTON BOOKS
A Division of the Collins Publishing Group

LONDON GLASGOW
TORONTO SYDNEY AUCKLAND

Paladin
Grafton Books
A Division of the Collins Publishing Group
8 Grafton Street, London W1X 3LA

Published in Paladin Books 1987
9 8 7 6 5 4 3 2

First published in Great Britain by
The Women's Press 1984

ISBN 0-586-08586-6

Printed and bound in Great Britain by
Collins, Glasgow

Set in Ehrhardt

This second volume is dedicated to
the Scrivener family, Frank Sargeson,
Karl and Kay Stead, and E. P. Dawson

Acknowledgements

Grateful acknowledgement to the New Zealand Literary Fund, Yaddo Corporation, and my friends. Grateful acknowledgement also to the following for permission to reprint selected passages: extract from 'The Stares Nest by My Window' by W. B. Yeats; Michael B. Yeats, Macmillan London Ltd and Macmillan Publishing Company, New York from 'The Poems' by W. B. Yeats, edited by Richard J. Finneran, copyright 1928 by Macmillan Publishing Company, Inc., renewed 1956 by George Yeats. Extracts from 'Great Sea, Kona Coast, Hawaii' and 'A View From Rangitoto' by Charles Brasch: Mr Alan Roddick and the Estate of Charles Brasch. Extract from 'Time' by Alan Curnow: the author. Extracts from 'Lamentation' from *Poems* by Lynette Roberts: Faber and Faber Ltd, London. Extract from 'Five Minutes More' by Jule Styne and Sammy Cahn: Morley Music Inc. Every effort has been made by the author and the publisher to trace other holders of copyright material.

Index of Chapters

PART ONE
Tricks of Desperation

Prospero: My brave spirit!
            Who was so firm, so constant, that this coil
            Would not infect his reason?

Ariel: Not a soul,
            But felt a fever of the mad; and play'd
            Some tricks of desperation.

Shakespeare, *The Tempest*, Act 1, Scene (ii).

1
The Stone

The future accumulates like a weight upon the past. The weight upon the earliest years is easier to remove to let that time spring up like grass that has been crushed. The years following childhood become welded to their future, massed like stone, and often the time beneath cannot spring back into growth like new grass: it lies bled of its green in a new shape with those frail bloodless sprouts of another, unfamiliar time, entangled one with the other beneath the stone.

2

Number Four Garden Terrace, Dunedin

The Sunday slow train, a goods train with a passenger carriage at the end, took seven hours to travel the seventy-eight miles between Oamaru and Dunedin, stopping at every station, waiting for at least half an hour by the gum trees at Waianakarua until the midday Limited rushed by on its way north, crawling by the wild-sweet-pea-surrounded sheds – the 'flag-stations' which I still ignorantly supposed to be named after the flag-lilies or swamp lilies, dark blue with pale white-blue throats specked with yellow, growing in the many swamps along the line. We stopped at Hampden where year after year we had travelled for the Railway Picnic, climbing from the train just before the cattlestop by the lagoon and its shadowy mass of black swans, walking higgledy-piggledy carrying kits and rugs down to the picnic ground by the beach with its beach 'dunny', the dark-stained wooden seat split down the middle, the concrete floor puddled muddy and salt-smelling, with here and there a splash of seagull mess as if the seagulls also used the changing-shed as a dunny. Now I, with memories created from the past as a foraging bee creates its own sweet architecture, looked out at Hampden and the black swans and the lagoon, remembering the sea and the beach of shells and the wet-floored dunny; and the railway raspberry drink, free.

Then followed the train's curious encircling of Palmerston with the stone monument on the hill appearing, disappearing, reappearing, with the few people in the carriage suddenly changing position, opening their windows, looking interested, for Palmerston was 'for refreshments', and the Limited had come and gone with its passengers, like locusts, eating through the supplies of ham sandwiches and sugar buns and hot pies, leaving only the 'stalks' for those on the goods train who were now seized, as everyone used to be at Palmerston, with hunger, and thirst.

The hills around Palmerston were burned by the sun and by fires, with only an occasional dead tree in a gully or half way up a slope, and now and again a cluster of trees, some long-dead, others shimmy-naked with only a thin layer of shiny leaves. More trees appeared as the train approached Seacliff and once again there was a movement in the carriage as the passengers became aware of *Seacliff*, the station, and *Seacliff* the hospital, the asylum, glimpsed as a castle of dark stone between the hills.

The train drew into the station. Yes, the loonies were there; everyone looked out at the loonies, known in Oamaru as those who were sent 'down the line', and in Dunedin, 'up the line'. Often it was hard to tell who were the loonies. A few people left the train here – they'd be the relations, visiting. We had no loonies in our family, although we knew of people who had been sent 'down the line', but we did not know what they looked like, only that there was a funny look in their eye and they'd attack you with a bread knife or an axe.

I was too fearful of the prospect of living in a big city like Dunedin, to pay much attention to Seacliff Station. The train now followed the winding track around the steep cliffs, looking down on the holiday settlements at Waitati, Karitane, where the 'group' at school had their 'cribs' by the sea where the world's mummys and daddys and big and little brothers and sisters had a life of fun with their beach and boats and sun and holiday games.

The train creaked, groaned, crawled, rocking, and the sea lay far below, calm and grey, slightly ruffled with a shine like a seal's fur. Then the tunnel, Mihiwaka, the passengers coughing, shutting and opening and shutting the windows, the carriage filled with smoke; out of the tunnel, the inescapable sense of arrival: Port Chalmers, Ravensbourne, Sawyers Bay; Dunedin Harbour and the Dunedin Railway Station, a huge, steaming, noisy place, not as crowded for the late afternoon arrival of the goods train as it would be for the Invercargill or Lyttelton Express, but still inspiring fear and awe: I was alone in my first city. My mind loomed with the fictions of the great cities of the world, and of Dunedin as such a city. I thought of the 'dark Satanic mills', of people 'caged like squirrels'; of fire, and plague and the press gang; and although I was willing to follow the example of the writers and eventually 'love' the new city, as Charles Dickens, Hazlitt, Lamb, loved their London, I could think first only of desolation, the poverty which I was sure I would find, and of how living in the city might destroy me –

We poets in our youth begin in gladness;
But thereof comes in the end despondency and madness.

I who had scarcely left childhood and who knew by heart Words-worth's 'Intimations of Immortality', had taken to myself the threat of

Full soon thy soul shall have her earthly freight,
And custom lie upon thee with a weight
Heavy as frost, and deep almost as life!

with the certainty that the threat would be realized in a big city: Dunedin. My consolation on that dreadful day of arrival lay in the prospect of my new home with Aunty Isy and Uncle George – Four Garden Terrace, a place of light with a terraced garden looking down over the bays of the peninsula, with my room, sharing the view, bright with cretonne curtains, a matching bedspread, and sheets on the bed as if for a princess. And I'd attend Training College, and University in my spare time, impressing people with my imagination; everyone would recognize me as a true poet. I'd not yet completed the practical details of a poet's life as I found it beyond even my imagination to make the transition from fantasy to fact – all the poets I'd studied were safely dead, and so long ago, in such distant countries, yet although I might not have determined my own way of life, it was the poets who kept me company on my first journey away from my home and family.

My knowledge of Aunty Isy and Uncle George was limited. I looked on them as I looked on most relatives and adults as 'formidable', living in a completely separate world where I could not imagine myself as belonging – the world of constant recitation of comings and goings of countless relatives and friends, of names of places, all spoken with the certainty of possession, of knowledge that each person was in a destined right place or if not there were questions and rumours as countless as the former affirmations. I knew Aunty Isy only as the former dancer in the old photographs of the two beautiful sisters Isabella and Polly dressed in their kilts, their waist-long black hair flowing behind them in strands of silk; as the aunt who held Myrtle, Dad's first-born, in all the photographs in which mother didn't appear, causing us to ask, 'Mum was Myrtle Aunty Isy's baby? Why weren't you photographed with baby Myrtle?'; as the kind aunt who sent a Christmas parcel each year, prompting the anxiety the week before Christmas, '*The parcel* hasn't arrived yet!'; and lately I thought of Aunty Isy as aunt-smelling of mothballs and cloth and wearing dark colours and working where she had worked all her life, now as supervisor in the Roslyn Mill; and still saying in a high voice, 'Lottie, Lottie, Middlemarch, Middlemarch.' And I thought of her husband, Uncle George, as a pale man in a grey overcoat; I think he was a commercial traveller.

Dunedin was half-hidden in misty rain. My taxi made a short journey from the railway station to half way up a hill street, Carroll Street, and there was Garden Terrace, and Number Four, the fourth small brick cottage in an attached group of six, their back and front doors reached by two narrow lanes from Carroll Street. Everywhere there were brick and concrete buildings, tall chimneys layered across the sky, grey streets, a view that I had seen in my mind's image of a city. Somewhere to the east was the sea which, ever faithful, had accompanied me from the kingdom of Oamaru.

Aunty Isy (aunt-smelling) hugged me at the door. She smelt of wardrobes full of clothing made of materials such as voile, jersey silk, serge, crepe-de-chine.

'Oh Jean, we're looking forward to your stay. We're all so proud you're going to be a teacher. We always look for your name in the paper at prize-giving; and the other girls, too. What a clever family!'

I stood smiling my shy smile which was more close-lipped than usual because my front teeth were now in the last stages of decay, as the Social Security Health Service did not allow for dentistry beyond primary school, and my family had no spare money to pay for dentists.

Aunty Isy's sisters-in-law, Molly and Elsie who lived next door at Number Five, and whom I knew as Aunty Molly (the radio aunt) and Aunty Elsie, came to say hello to me.

'So this is Jean, and you're going to be a teacher?'

'Yes.'

The cottage was like a large doll's house, with a tiny scullery with sink-bench just inside the back door, a sitting-dining room, known as the 'wee' room next to it along a narrow passageway, with another slightly larger room, the 'best' sitting room just inside the front door. Upstairs there were two bedrooms, both small. The bathroom was downstairs in the wash-house leading from the scullery.

'Your room is up here,' Aunty Isy said, 'at the top of the stairs.'

As we walked up the stairs she turned to the right to the room where she and Uncle George slept.

'Uncle George is in bed,' she explained. 'Would you like to say hello to him?'

I knew that Uncle George had cancer. I stood at the end of the bed.

'George, Jean has come to say hello to you.'

'Hello, Uncle George.'

'So you're the one who's going to be a teacher?'

I noted the grey pallor of his face with its soft-looking skin, like dead skin, and I wondered what dreadful sight was concealed beneath the bedclothes. There was an oily smell of lanoline, and a row of blue and white empty lanoline tubes, some squashed and rolled up, on the dressing-table. Sexually curious as well as ignorant, I wondered if the lanoline had anything to do with 'it', and I wondered if Aunty Isy and Uncle George 'did it'.

Perhaps you couldn't, if you had cancer?

'He spends most of his time in bed now,' Aunty Isy said, as we went downstairs for our cup of tea.

Later, I sat on my bed in my tiny room that looked out over brick walls, miles of buildings with tall chimneys. If I leaned out the window I could see, just inside the front gate into the alley, the small garden blooming with geraniums which I had not thought of before as city flowers; they were dusty with soot layered over their own flame-velvet. I felt a stirring of anticipation and excitement as I realized that I was alone in my first grey city; then gradually the excitement gave way to anxiety. So this was how it was, face to face with the Future – being alone, having no-one to talk to, being afraid of the city and Training College and teaching, and having to pretend that I was not alone, that I had many people to talk to, that I felt at home in Dunedin, and that teaching was what I had longed to do all my life.

3
The Student

My first week at Dunedin Training College was less painful than I had expected, for I shared my newness with many others, all apprehensive, all anxious to learn quickly the assured student ways, while the lecturers, not as remote as the adults I had previously known, amazed me by their insight as they explained our feelings, trying to fit us comfortably into the role of students. They called us Mr and Miss, with an occasional Mrs, but because the War had not ended, there were few men, who were quickly claimed by the beautiful blonde women while the rest, myself among them, survived by daydreaming of what might be and by concentrating admiration on the most handsome lecturers.

I had my first adventure in assurance when I heard the new language which I would soon speak but which I now approached with awe and with the fear of intimate reference and abbreviation. While the other new students were saying casually, *Training Coll, Varsity, Party* (for Mr Partridge, the Principle), *Crit Lesson*, I still could not bring myself to utter the magical words. The gradual learning of the language, the attitudes, customs of behaviour and dress, produced in me a euphoria of belonging which was intensified and contradicted by my actual feeling of isolation. At the Thursday morning Assembly while we waited for the appearance of the staff and *Party*, the second-year students began singing 'their' song which was soon to be 'ours'. My heart turned over with the momentous import of the occasion as the second-year students sang,

> Oh the deacon went down
> Oh the deacon went down

to the cellar to pray
and he darn got drunk
and he stayed all day (and he stayed all day)
Oh the deacon went down
to the cellar to pray
and he darn got drunk
and he stayed all day,
Oh I ain't gonna grieve my Lord no more . . .

Oh the devil he's got (Oh the devil he's got)
a hypocrite shoe . . .
If you want to go to hell and burn in fire
just don't you do the Lord's desire . . .

I found the joyous singing as moving as if it had been an extract from the *Messiah*, performed by every choral society every Christmas and so familiar to those not directly in touch with that kind of music. The idea that soon I, too, would be singing, 'Oh the deacon went down' (there were even a few now among the first-years who had joined the chorus) seemed to me like a promise of heaven. Everyone was laughing and talking and excited and everywhere the new language was being spoken with such certainty and power!

Then, when Party and his staff appeared, the singing stopped, and everyone, even the staff, wore a look of self-satisfaction as if they shared a tremendous secret, as if student life were the happiest of all.

Later I saw two ex-Waitakians, Katherine Bradley and Rona Pinder.

'College is fun,' they said.

I agreed. 'Yes, isn't it?'

During that first week, making plans to study English and French at University with the Education Department paying my fees, I was interviewed by Mr Partridge who also lectured in Education. I remember him as a small neat dark man in a dark suit. His aura of power came from his role of Principal who, I had heard, pinned notes on the message board, requesting an interview, and none knew, although some suspected, whether a 'note from Party' would result in praise or condemnation.

Mr Partridge asked about my accommodation.

'Do you live in one of the hostels?'

'I stay with an aunt and uncle.'

He frowned.

'It's not always good to stay with relatives.'

'Oh, I get on well with my aunt and uncle. And I pay only ten shillings board.'

'Where do you live?'

'Four Garden Terrace, Carroll Street.'

He frowned again.

'Carroll Street? That's not a very nice area.'

I knew that Carroll Street was two streets from the notorious McLaggan Street where prostitutes were said to live, and the Chinese to smoke opium in their opium 'dens', but Carroll Street seemed harmless to me: I had found that it was known as the 'Syrian quarter'.

'Not a savoury area at all,' Mr Partridge repeated disapprovingly, giving no explanation for his opinion.

'So you want to study English and French?'

He consulted some papers on his desk, and frowned again, 'I suppose you realize that doing well at school doesn't mean you'll do well at University. There are students from all over the country here, you know. And Training College is a full time course.'

Subdued, I nodded. 'Yes.'

He persisted.

'In fact several students who did well at school have failed their University subjects.'

Reluctantly he gave me permission to study Stage One English and French, and with his disapproval tearing painfully at the perfect edge of my newfound world, I left his office and walked home down Union Street, through the Museum Grounds to Frederick Street, into George Street, past the Octagon, into Princes Street, and into Carroll Street to my newly unsavoury address. I still could not see, however, why Carroll Street was not 'nice'. The people were poorer, there were few who went to Training College or University, and sometimes, perhaps, there were a few more drunks outside the pub at six-o'clock closing . . .

I found myself defeated in coping with the initial requisite of belonging to Training College: the building was new and I was afraid of its newness, its nakedness. I had never occupied such a clean place. Unlike at High School where each class had its own room which was treated as 'home' for the day, the rooms at the Training College were distinguished by subjects – the Education Room, the Art Room – with the only 'home' for the students being their lockers in the locker room where possessions and not people could be housed. The 'home' for the students was the *Common Room* diminished in security for me by the vast space of its floor and its very newness, though I was delighted to be able to say at last, with the old dreams of University, Oxford, Cambridge, 'The Scholar Gypsy', *Jude the Obscure*, still burning in my mind, *Common Room. I shall go to the Common Room. They are in the Common Room.* In reality, I rarely used the Common Room.

I was overawed, too, by the lavatories. Near the wash-basin was an incinerator with a sign, *Deposit Used Sanitary Towels Here.* One had to walk, with soiled sanitary towel in hand for all to see, from the lavatory, across the tiled echoing floor, to the incinerator at the far end of the room. In my two years at Training College I carried my soiled sanitary towels home to Number Four Garden Terrace to put in the wash-house dustbin when Aunty Isy was out, or to throw among the tombstones in the Southern Cemetery at the top of the street which had become my place to 'be', to think, to compose poems, my Dunedin equivalent of the 'hill' at Oamaru. During the weekend when Aunty Isy lit the dining room fire and asked discreetly if I had 'anything to burn', I'd say, 'No, thank you.'

'Yes please.' 'No thank you.'

My few clothes shared the dressing-table drawer with used sanitary towels waiting to be thrown in the cemetery and with the wrappers from the bars of Caramello chocolate which I ate in my room. In my anxiety to be thought the perfect boarder, from the beginning of my stay I had explained to Aunty Isy that I ate very little, that I was a vegetarian (I had been studying Buddhism), and would be content to have my small meal on the sink-bench in the scullery, and when Aunty Isy reminded me that I was welcome to eat in the dining room, I, excessively timid, made the excuse that I liked to study while I ate. Now, when I was less afraid of the city and was even learning to ride the tramcars, I was unable to revise my impression as the girl with the tiny appetite, and so I was often hungry. I'd grab delicious scraps of boiled corned beef, set aside as being 'too stringy', from Aunty Isy's plate among the pile of dirty dishes. And I bought the Caramello chocolate, a shilling a bar, to eat in my room.

I took little part in College social life. I yearned for the time when I could buy a crumpled gaberdine raincoat (the student uniform). In complete ignorance of the ways of love and sex, I watched with envious wonder the lives of those women who, finding their 'man', fulfilled not only their own expectations but those of their family and friends and thus added a bloom of certainty to their being. My only romance was with poetry and literature, at Training College lectures, and those newly begun at University where I spent my dreaming-time. At University I was not called on to behave like a teacher. I could sit in the lecture room listening, not even asked to speak, dreaming unhindered by criticism or comment about the subject of the lecture and, at times, the lecturer. My concentration was intense. I marvelled at all the new knowledge, the enthusiasm and talent of the lecturers both at Training College and University, at the new language, each distinct, of Training College students and University students, and, in the English classes taken by Professor Ramsay and Gregor Cameron, at the newly presented language of Shakespeare and Chaucer, with Professor Ramsay analyzing each word of Shakespeare, transmitting to us his own sense of wonder at Shakespeare's language and its meaning. Like the sea from Oamaru, Shakespeare and his language travelled with me to Dunedin and were treasured for sharing my new life and the life of 'the girl that was gone'. We studied *Measure for Measure*, which I had never read but which now became one of my favourite Shakespeare plays, with every line stirring in me a host of ideas crowding avenues of dreaming, lines of poems, the end-of-term examination papers, but not, to my regret, the literary essays I had longed to write. It was not then the way of University lecturers to ask for written or spoken comment from Stage I or Stage II students. In Training College English assignments I was able now and then to satisfy my desire to write prose.

Many of my student days and experiences are now sealed from me by that substance released with the life of each moment or each moment's capture of our life. I remember and can relive my feelings but there is now a thirst for reason in what had seemed to be so inevitable. I did not realize the extent of my loneliness. I clung to works of literature as a child clings to its mother. I remember how *Measure for Measure*, the deeply reasoned play crammed with violations of innocence, with sexual struggle and comment, with long discussions on life, death and immortality, won my heart and persisted in my memory, *accompanied* me in my daily life:

> What's yet in this that bears the name of life? Yet in this
> life lie hid more thousand deaths; yet death we fear.

It is a stark play of honest language, of comfort and remedy, analysis of revenge and payment and life and death set in the scales. Writing now, I am impatient with my student self that was so unformed, ungrownup, so cruelly innocent. Although I had no means of knowing if other students lived in such innocence, I have since learned that many, in timidity and shyness and ignorance, lived as bizarre a life as I. I have heard of others who made detours along the bush-covered Town Belt to dispose of sanitary towels; and of one women who spent her first week in a student hostel in darkness because she was too timid to ask for a light bulb to be replaced, and she had no money to buy one. Our lives were frail, full of agonies of embarrassment and regret, of misunderstood communication and strong with the intense feeling of wonder at the torrent of ideas released by books, music, art, other people; it was a time of finding shelter among the mightily capitalled abstractions of Love, Life, Time, Age, Youth, Imagination.

The Southern Cemetery where I threw my embarrassing litter was my favourite place. I was too shy to sit with Aunty Isy in the small dining room by the fire, and when the view of brick walls and desolate backyards and their overflowing rubbish tins became too depressing I climbed the hill and sitting in the long grass or on one of the walled graves, I looked out over my new city – Caversham and the grey stone building like a workhouse which I first thought might be the *Industrial School* but later I found to be *Parkside*, a home for old people, the 'Railway' end of Carisbrook football ground, the Oval with its weekday rainwater puddles and seagulls; crowded, poor, flood-prone St Kilda where I had lived for the first six weeks of my life. I looked out over the peninsula too and the waters of the harbour, and beyond, to the open sea, the Pacific, *my* Pacific.

My Pacific, *my* city: in my own way, I was making friends. Sitting among the old dead of old Dunedin (for the new dead had a special place, a headland overlooking the sea at Anderson's Bay), I earned or stole a little of their peace, there in the softly-blowing long grass among the onion flowers and the wild sweet peas and the deep-rooted dock that used to be part of cemeteries, the accessories of both the railway lines and the dead. I'd compose a poem to write later when I returned to Garden Terrace. And as I walked by the telephone box at the top of the street, suddenly it would seem that the company of the dead was not enough, and one evening I telephoned Miss Macaulay who had retired from Waitaki and was living with her elderly mother at St Clair. When she answered I found I had nothing to say yet I clung to the phone, putting in penny after penny as each three minutes wore away. I telephoned several times during the early months of my stay in Dunedin. The habit was killed abruptly one evening when Miss Macaulay said, 'You've spent one shilling, Jean!'

I had not realized that she could hear the money being fed into the box. My shame was intense. I did not dare admit my feeling of isolation. I had said again and again how wonderful it was, Training College and University. And the French classes? (Miss Macaulay had taught English and French.) Oh, I so much enjoyed them! That was true – both the English and French classes sustained me in my new life of a student teacher. I did not phone St Clair again.

A few weeks after that Katherine Bradley, Rona Pinder, and I, three of Miss Macaulay's 'old girls' accepted her invitation to afternoon tea at her home. We drank tea and ate slices of chocolate cake with chocolate icing in a house padded with cushions and dark furniture: an ordinary house. We talked of our studies and exchanged greetings with old Mrs Macaulay, all in the presence of the 'shadow' falling between the 'ideal and the real'. I had thought that our teacher, retiring, would continue her study of French and English literature, would perhaps write essays. Our conversation was unenlightening. I was haunted by the idea that all our teaching at school had been a pretence, that the great literature had been *endured* rather than *enjoyed*, then cast aside for worldly matters. Could that have been? I felt betrayed. Yet I knew that my teachers at University would persist in their studies until they died. Professor Ramsay and Gregor Cameron could never be imagined apart from Shakespeare and Chaucer.

Might they have been separated from their literature if they had an elderly mother to care for, if they were women? I was saddened by the knowledge that Miss Macaulay had been extracted from her place by the same domesticity that had denied my mother a sight of hers.

'Come and visit me again,' Miss Macaulay said.

I did not go again.

My visits home became fewer. I'd buy a privilege ticket to travel on the Friday night train arriving at Oamaru between one and two in the morning, returning to Dunedin by the Sunday slow train. On the way home I'd imagine that all would be peaceful, different, at 56 Eden Street, but as soon as I arrived I wished I had not come. Isabel and June were busy with their own lives, the antagonism between my father and my brother had increased, while mother, self-effacing, maintained her role of provider of food, peacemaker, poet, with a new dream to add to 'publication' and the Second Coming of Christ – a dream that set her among the characters in fairy tales – that each of her daughters, now grown, should have a white fox fur on her twenty-first birthday. Her dream for Bruddie, for health or fame in spite of ill-heath, was unchanged.

My dissatisfaction with my home and family was intense. The ignorance of my parents infuriated me. They knew nothing of

Sigmund Freud, of *The Golden Bough*, of T. S. Eliot. (I forgot, conveniently, that at the beginning of the year my knowledge of Freud, *The Golden Bough*, T. S. Eliot, was limited.) Overwhelmed with the flood of new knowledge I was bursting with information about the Mind, the Soul, the Child, both the Normal Child and the Young Delinquent, where I had only recently learned that there was such a creature as *The Child*. All were described, measured, labelled, expounded in detail to my bewildered parents. I was equally enthusiastic about my new knowledge of Agricultural Science and Geomorphology. I talked of compost and rock formations. I explained theories as if they were my own. I had accepted the opinions on the classification of people partly because I was dazzled by the new language and its powerful vocabulary. I could now say to members of my family, 'That's rationalization, that's sublimation, you're really frustrated sexually, your super-ego tells you that but your Id disagrees.'

Mother blushed when I said the word 'sexually'. Dad frowned, and said nothing except, 'So that's what you learn at University and Training College.'

I explained to my sisters the significance of their dreams, how 'everything was phallic'. I also talked with exaggerated wisdom of T. S. Eliot and *The Golden Bough* and 'The Waste Land'. 'I love teaching,' I said, explaining how we had a month in College, a month in schools, how there were crit lessons, days of control, when we had the class by ourselves for one day, how we had a report at the end of the month.

'Aunty Isy says you're a lovely girl,' mother said proudly. 'She says you're no trouble at all, she scarcely knows you're in the house.'

'Oh well,' I said, pleased that both she and Dad were pleased.

'And it's a help to have you in the house, with Uncle George ill.'

Uncle George. Well, that was a mystery. Sometimes he got out of bed and went for a walk, I didn't know where, but he wore a grey overcoat and went out into the grey night and when he came home his face was grey, too, and Aunty Isy would help him off with his coat, unwind his scarf, and see him up to bed, perhaps calling down the stairs, 'Jean would you mind running down to Joe the Syrian's for a tube of lanoline?'

And once again I'd fetch the blue and white tube of lanoline.

'And how *is* Uncle George?' mother asked. (I had begun to call 'Mum' 'mother' as a sign that I was grown up.)

'I don't really know,' I said. 'He goes for a walk sometimes. Nobody mentions his illness.'

I knew they were pretending he was not ill. I hated the pretence. I hated being home, for I felt that I had left home forever, and except for occasional visits, I would never return. I could see the family so clearly enveloped in doom that it frightened me. I felt that my mother lived in a world which in no way corresponded with the 'real' world, and it seemed that her every word was a concealment, a lie, a desperate refusal to acknowledge 'reality'. I was not even aware that I, in my turn, had joined the world of pretence which I so condemned in others.

I could see my father as a helpless character struggling against the buffeting winds of a cruel world. In my mind I could see him as he rode his bicycle up the slope of Eden Street, his body leaning forward, determined not to give in to the hill and the head wind blowing straight from the snow, from up country, 'out Hakataramea way' towards the Southern Alps; and my brother, fresh-faced with his brown hair sticking up like Uncle Bob's hair, and his mouth tremulous with all those tears he had shed in his helplessness against his attacker; and my sisters – Isabel growing so like Myrtle in her nature, defiant, daring, a rebel and everybody's darling; and June, in the blue Wilson House girdle that somehow suited her quietness, full of vague poetry and music and most likely to share my tastes in reading and to understand my musings on the Great Abstractions – all my family were part of the shared 'we' which I knew to be lost. I tried to use 'we' when I talked of my life as a student, but I knew it was futile, that I was describing what 'they', the students did, where they went, how they felt, what they said, and in order to survive I had to conceal my 'I', what I really felt, thought, and dreamed about. I had moved from the second person plural to a shadowy 'I', almost a nothingness, like a no-woman's land.

I was named a 'student', 'one of them', complained about by the public of Dunedin, referred to affectionately or reprovingly by the lecturers as 'Oh, you students!', or proudly by my relatives as 'A student, you know.' Sensing the excitement and pleasure of my fellow students in all the activities – drama, sport, debating, dancing, 'going out' with the opposite sex, I found myself almost delirious with excitement at the contemplation of the life of a student. I must have spent a fortune of dazzlement and wonderment, simply in knowing that I was *there*; and few experiences could have equalled the joy given by being at a University, perceived by me almost entirely through English literature – surely Gregor Cameron was the Grammarian of 'A Grammarian's Funeral'?

> Here – here's his place where meteors shoot, clouds form,
> Lightnings are loosened,
> Stars come and go! let joy break with the storm,
> Peace let the dew send!
> Lofty designs must close in like effects;
> Loftily lying,
> Leave him – still loftier than the world suspects,
> Living and dying.

Little did Gregor Cameron know that in the midst of 'Beowulf' and 'Piers Plowman', he stood on the platform in Lower Oliver, the English room, as Browning's 'Grammarian' – 'our master, famous calm and dead.'

Everything was furiously swift, relentless; even the venerable stone walls of the University swirled with secret life, but where human life was being lived, openly, as in the Common Room and the Canteen, I was always afraid to venture. The student weekly newspaper, *Critic*, was set just outside the door of the University Student Union building, with an invitation, 'Take One'. Only three or four times during my life as a student was I bold enough to take a copy of *Critic*. With so much freedom how could I have been so confined by myself? I longed to be brave enough to submit a poem to *Critic*. When I eagerly caught the crumb-pages discarded on a desk or chair in the corridor, I studied the stories and poems and dreamed of seeing my poems printed, myself *speaking out* boldly, brilliantly, in denial of my timidity, isolation, and fear of The World. I knew that inside the Student Union building there was a postbox inviting contributions: I was not brave enough to enter the Student Union building. Although I dreamed of writing poems that would startle and satisfy with their brilliance, I knew that I had not the talent, the assurance, the wonderful maturity that spoke so clearly in the poetry pages of *Critic*. Everyone was writing free verse, discarding capital letters and punctuation, often leaping into the poem with the object only, 'Dreamed . . . tall sky, lowering . . .' etc.

Also there were favourite words used with certainty – cornucopia, thighs, phallic, molls, deathless, wordless, breathless, the eye, the heart, the mind, the womb; tough poems full of experience, one moment laconic, the next profuse. Heavily under the influence of John Donne, the men wrote poems about women, tangled metaphorical exchanges of hearts, beds, souls, bodies, while the women wrote of flowers, forests, the sea. Influenced by the 'sprung rhythm' of Hopkins and the vocabulary of Dylan Thomas, I wrote mysterious poems full of images derived from my past and tributary pasts, and my present, all focused through my newly-acquired Freudian lens with its tint of T. S. Eliot's geraniums growing in the Waste Land and at Number Four Garden Terrace, and dead, shaken by a madman.

Always, as my mother had done, I allied myself with the poets. I adopted extravagant beliefs. After learning Shelley

> True love in this differs from gold and clay
> That to divide is not to take away.
> Love is like understanding that grows bright
> Gazing on many truths, 'tis like thy light,
> *Imagination!* which from earth and sky,
> And from the depths of human fantasy . . .

I announced to myself and to anyone who might be interested that I 'believed' in 'free love' and 'polygamy' – I, grasping the abundance when I was not even in sight of the pittance! ·

The most magical word to me was still *Imagination*, a glittering noble word never failing to create its own inner light. I was learning much about its composition from the University studies of the 'set book', Coleridge's *Biographia Literaria*. I learned by heart the passage,

The Imagination then I consider either as primary or secondary. The primary Imagination I hold to be the living Power and prime Agent of all human Perception, and as a repetition in the finite mind of the eternal act of creation in the infinite I am. The secondary Imagination I consider as an echo of the former, co-existing with the conscious will, yet still as identical with the primary in the *kind* of its agency, and differing only in *degree* and in the *mode* of its operation. It dissolves, diffuses, dissipates, in order to recreate; or where this process is rendered impossible, yet still at all events it struggles to idealize and to unify. It is essentially *vital*, even as all objects (*as* objects) are essentially fixed and dead . . . Fancy, on the contrary, has no other counters to play with, but fixities and definites. The Fancy if indeed no other than a mode of Memory emancipated from the order of time and space; while it is blended with and modified by that empirical phenomenon of the will, which we express by the word Choice. But equally with the ordinary memory the Fancy must receive all its materials ready made from the law of association. Good sense is the body of poetic genius, Fancy its drapery, Motion its life, and Imagination the soul that is everywhere and in each; and forms all into one graceful and intelligent whole.

I was fascinated by the implied gap, the darkness, the Waste Land between Fancy and Imagination, and the lonely journey when the point of Fancy had been passed and only Imagination lay ahead. It became my goal, a kind of religion. No-one had ever forbidden association with or frowned on, Imagination, and although I had few illusions about my own share, I held it in my secret poetic life, it flowed between the poetry and prose I read and myself, and even the probable mockery of others or my own more likely self-mockery with 'frustration', 'sublimation', could not hurt or destroy it for it was, as Coleridge and all the poets had said, 'supreme', and at that time of my life when I was learning that life is a presentation of many feasts from which one is often fearful of being turned away, I found the feast of imagination spread almost in loving fashion, in great kindness and abundance.

The War continued. I worried about my decayed teeth, my

clothes, money, teaching. On pay day, cashing my cheque for nine pounds three and ninepence, at Arthur Barnetts, I went with other students to the *Silver Grille* for a 'mixed grille please.' Some of the students even drank *coffee*. They – we – the quieter ones – talked of the wild exploits of certain other students, enviously noting who 'went with' a medical student, for medical students were said to 'know everything' about sex. 'Let me show you your spare rib,' they'd say.

And the War continued, giving an air of unreality layered upon the ordinary air of unreality, forming an atmosphere of sadness, pity, helplessness. The everlasting question was Why.

At Number Four Garden Terrace, Uncle George's pallor changed to the grey of approaching death. He no longer went out walking or came downstairs to visit Aunty Isy in the sitting room, and talk to her and to Billy the Budgerigar who could say, Pretty Boy, Pretty Boy, Billy, Up the stairs to bed, up the stairs to bed. More and more tubes of lanoline were emptied and disposed of. Before I went to my room I'd say hello to Uncle George, standing at the foot of the bed, scanning his concealed shape for signs of the cancer which he and Aunty Isy guarded so closely and fed so lavishly on Sharlands Lanoline.

Then one Sunday when I returned from walking in the cemetery, Aunty Isy met me at the door.

'Uncle George has passed away, Jean.'

I had not known him. Uncle George the commercial traveller who had once lived at Middlemarch. Middlemarch. Middlemarch. The way Aunty Isy used to say it, I thought she owned Middlemarch and the world, but it was Uncle George she owned. And although I did not even love him, confronted by his dying, I felt a wild grief and, bursting into tears, I ran upstairs to my room. I did not go to College the next day, and when Mr Partridge asked me to explain my absence I said, consciously adopting a sad voice fitting for grief, 'My uncle died in the weekend and I stayed home to help my aunt.'

Uncle George's sisters had taken him next door to Number Five, for the funeral, and I had the feeling that a long-lasting

31

dispute about the possession of Uncle George had been settled by his removal next door.

The big bed in the room next to mine was covered with a new spring-bright bedspread while the dustbin where I sneaked to dispose of wrappers and sanitary towels was packed with the familiar blue and white empty tubes.

Aunty Isy was still silent about the illness and the death. She took little time off work, a day of two to tidy the house and wash or burn a bundle of bed-linen. Sometimes her face and eyes had a dusky look, like that of grief when there are no tears being shed. But she still talked of *Middlemarch*, reinvesting it with the feeling that now had nowhere else to go.

4

Again 'A Country Full of Rivers'

I kept the continuing War within the boundaries of Modern Literature, and when a new student would arrive, slightly older, limping, with one leg or one arm, I viewed him from the safety of myth as 'the old soldier home from the Wars'. I emerged blinking from the half-dark of Dostoievski, the star and sky-filled grandeur of Thomas Hardy's world with the isolating, oppressing, indifferent hand of doom upon each character, that is, from the writers who were dead, to discover there were writers who were only recently dead or who were living and writing in the midst of the War. I read James Joyce, Virginia Woolf, the poetry of Auden, Barker, MacNeice, Laura Riding (noting that she had been the wife of Robert Graves), and – Dylan Thomas, the hero, then, I'm sure, of every student who read or wrote poetry. I bought the *Poems* of Sydney Keyes, and took much time to gaze at his photograph and mourn his early death. I treasured a small volume of T. S. Eliot, a large anthology, *Poetry London*, with drawings by Henry Moore and writing by Henry Miller, and my *Poetry in Wartime* where, isolated from our own casualty lists and the deaths of young men we'd known in Oamaru, brothers or sons of neighbours, I lived within the air raids on London, the routine of the fire-watchers and the Air-Raid Wardens – many of the poems had been written 'while fire-watching'. I knew by heart Auden's 'September 1, 1939', poems on the 'Four Seasons of War', Lynette Roberts' 'Lamentation':

> Five hills rocked and four homes fell
> the day I remember the raid so well.
> Eyes shone like cups chipped and stiff,

the living bled, the dead lay in their grief.
Dead as ice-bone breaking the hedge,
dead as soil failing of good heart.
Dead as trees quivering with shock
at the hot death from the plane.

There was a national activity known as the *War Effort* which
touched my life, as all were expected to take part. During the
summer of that year other students and I were 'manpowered' to
pick raspberries on Whittakers' farm at Millers Flat, Central Otago.
I was excited by the idea of going 'up Central' to the place that had
haunted me since infancy when I thought of it as a tall ladder with
narrow rungs where aunts and uncles climbed up one side into the
clouds, stayed the weekend or longer, then came down, saying
with great satisfaction, 'I've been up Central.'

The reality was a journey in an old bus along dusty roads set in
a moonscape of burned bare hills rising almost perpendicularly
from the valleys, to a fertile plain by the banks of a turbulent green
churned-white river, there known as the Molyneux, but further
downstream as the Clutha. From my first sight of the river I felt it
to be a part of my life (how greedily I was claiming the features of
the land as 'part of my life'), from its beginning in the snow of the
high country (we were almost in the high country), through all its
stages of fury and, reputedly now and then, peace, to its outfall in
the sea, with its natural burden of water and motion and its display
of colour, snowgreen, blue, mud-brown, and borrowing rainbows
from light; and its added burden, rising from its power, of the
dead – withered or uprooted vegetation, the bodies and bones of
cattle, sheep and deer; and, from time to time, of people who
drowned.

After spending a year confined in the city, studying, writing,
conscious always of boundaries of behaviour and feeling, in my
new role as an adult, I now came face to face with the Clutha, a
being that persisted through all the pressures of rock, stone, earth
and sun, living as an element of freedom but not isolated, linked to
heaven and light by the slender rainbow that shimmered above its
waters. I felt the river was an ally, that it would speak for me.

I fell in love with Central Otago and the river, with the naked

34

hills covered only in their folds by their own shadow, with their changing shades of gold, and the sky born each morning with no trace of cloud, retiring in the evening to its depth of purple. Day and night we tried to endure the heat of the sun burning the air outside and stored in the corrugated iron walls and roof of the large shed where we lived and slept. Every day, all day, we picked raspberries as we'd been taught, crouched, milking them gently from their stalks, dropping the soft furry blobs into the tin bucket hanging by a cord around our neck. Our hands were stained with raspberry blood, and scratched with raspberry thorns that, singly, were soft to the touch, but massed against the stem could pierce like pins. My face and arms and legs flamed with sunburn. I was a slow picker, earning barely enough to pay my fare home to Oamaru.

The pickers, coming from strange places like Whakatane, Matamata, Tuatapere, seemed to me like goddesses, fascinating in everything they said and did. The farmer's sons were like younger gods: I watched their faces, their eyes, studied their hands, arms, legs, glancing briefly but often at the bulge, the snowball bedded in snowgrass, between their legs. The world was a feast with nothing denied except by the marking of the invisible boundaries: we were not rivers. The other students, the one or two whom I knew, were overpowered by their surroundings, by the knowledge of the War, by their own uncertainties. We were now half way through our training as teachers: would we succeed? How would it be, in our senior year? There was the Social Studies Assignment rumoured to take all year to write and (some said) expected to be the length of a book. And how would we fare in the year of 'C' Certificate? And what of our love-life? We talked about longing and love, told our love-lorn dreams of those unattainable too few male students – miners, medical men – of our clinging to chance kind words that, falling on too receptive ears, inspired the right to repeat the melting poetry of

> My true-love hath my heart, and I have his,
> By just exchange one for the other given.

In the evening I walked on the hill, among the matagouri, a desert thorn bush with ragged stunted growth and small grey leaves like tarnished flakes of snow. I fell in love with matagouri, for though it grew on the hills around Oamaru, its name was new to me, given by one of the gods or goddesses in answer to my question, What is this marvellous plant? Matagouri (tumutakuru) grew its marvel overnight into my newly awakened world. I found, too, on the hills, a grass I'd not seen since early childhood – snowgrass, golden silk like the strands of tussock which I used to think was named after 'tussore' silk, a dreamed-of material out of my past where school blouses were rayon or cotton and only the privileged few wore 'tussore' silk, the colour of cream with coarse threads electric to the touch in the midst of the noisy softness. I remembered how Myrtle had maintained a fantasy that she had a 'tussore silk dress' hanging in the wardrobe, and how she would skite about it, 'I've got a dress of tussore silk.'

That summer was a time of the dominion of sun, of love to give everywhere in feeling that could not be matched by the past written word: the agony, the rapture, the still-innocent longing, the painful pleasure and pleasurable pain (we had 'studied' the 'pleasure-pain principle'); the memory remains, for me, in the bounty of the river and the landscape, the matagouri and snowgrass, the flawless blue of the sky, set beside the nightmare of the burning corrugated iron enclosing us with its fire.

I returned home, my summer love slowly cooling. I understood why relatives had voiced their rapture about 'up Central' and how as an infant I had seen 'up Central' as a ladder into heaven.

At 56 Eden Street the parched front lawn was scattered with dry cocksfoot seeds and faded tinker-tailor grass. There was ergot, too, to be collected for the War Effort; and in the bull paddock, rambler rose-bushes laden with rose-hips about to ripen.

Isabel and I lay on the lawn while I, the big sister, explained how it was at Training College and Isabel listened with her usual scepticism. She was preparing for her First Year. Both she and I would be staying with Aunty Isy at Number Four Garden Terrace. I felt a sense of panic at the idea of having to 'cope' with Isabel.

5

Isabel and the Growth of Cities

Although Isabel and I were good friends we were almost opposite in our behaviour, outlook, experience and ambitions. It was Isabel who instructed June and me in the 'ways of the world', that is, how to get a boyfriend, what to do when you had him and how to get rid of him when he outlived his usefulness; how to be beautiful in complexion and figure to make certain you did get your boyfriend; and how to triumph over authority and its narrow-mindedness. Isabel was inclined to teach us by example: her social experiences were many; she always had a boyfriend; she described in detail what they did together and although she hadn't yet gone 'all the way' she explained vividly what happened, with a mixture of fiction and fact accompanied by the favourite song of the time, sung by Fats Waller in a throaty voice,

> Please don't put your lips so close to my cheek,
> Don't smile or I'll be lost beyond recall
> ... *all or nothing at all* ...

Isabel was imaginative, clever, topping her school class in English and French and winning the Speech Prize and a Physical Education Shield; she also collected a place in an earlier long jump championship. Even in our competitive world we did not overvalue these awards; they gave prestige, however, and often came with a handsome book or medal or a cheque.

I envied Isabel her power of written description, the supply of detail gathered entirely from her imagination which made her seem to me to have travelled the world and lived in many times and places; she simply *knew*. When her ambition to be a doctor was curbed by her impatience with study and the cost of training, she decided to try teaching, even without spending time in the Sixth Form.

I, self-concious, restrained, obedient, thinking of myself as responsible and grown up, felt alarm at Isabel's very first move – coming to Training College '*straight from the Fifth Form*' without a year or two years enduring the Sixth Form as a kind of 'discipline for life'. I saw my own world falling apart, all my carefully cemented behaviour crumbling under the force of Isabel's unexpected weather. It was hard work studying both at Training College and University, and with the Social Studies Assignment (the subject already given – 'The Growth Of Cities') supposed to be the length of a book, I could not see how I could 'fit in' Isabel and my apprehension about her survival. My habit of behaving as I was expected to behave – 'obedient, no trouble at all', and my absorption in the world of literature, enabled me to enjoy living a monastic life because no matter how I might desire to be distracted along the way, my pursuit was poetry. My view forward was narrow, and when I glanced aside at others going their different ways, my view remained narrow. I wanted Isabel to be as the dolls had been (clothes-pegs wrapped in cloth) when we pressed them into tiny boxes and kept them there, safely wrapped and snug, able to move only with our help. I wanted her to be a good student, to 'behave', to obey, to study and be approved of by the students and the lecturers, perhaps, though I did not voice this to myself, causing the Principal to say, 'We made no mistake admitting those Frame girls to Training College, they're two of our best students and teachers.' Aunty Isy, expecting another meek Frame who would do her best to be invisible and accept, uncomplaining, the conditions which I myself had set, welcomed Isabel to stay, and when we arrived at Four Garden Terrace and Isabel and I were alone in the small room that we were to share, Isabel was angrily incredulous at the thought of sharing the two-foot-six wide iron bed with me. It had been my fault: I had said timidly, 'Oh that will be quite alright,' when Aunty Isy asked if we could manage.

'But even her thinking of it,' Isabel said angrily.

38

'Oh don't say anything,' I said, pacifying Isabel. We both knew there was nowhere else to stay at ten shillings a week.

We had little sleep, we were constantly irritated, quarrelling with each other, fighting over our share of the bedclothes, as we used to do at home. Horrified at the uncomplaining way I accepted our tiny ration of food, eating it at the bench in the scullery, Isabel threatened to 'tell Mum' that Aunty Isy was starving us, that she made us eat in the scullery, and sleep in a tiny bed in a tiny room scarcely big enough to swing a cat in, that we were frozen night and day with that cold wind blowing fresh from the harbour or down North-East Valley from Flagstaff and the outlying hills, while Aunty Isy ate in her dining room and toasted her toes in front of a blazing fire.

I persuaded Isabel not to say anything.

'Not just now, wait till the end of term.'

In Isabel's first weeks at Training College she made friends, she found a boyfriend, who became her 'steady' while she was there, although from time to time she had others, and she behaved as I had dreaded she would; she went 'wild', with a wildness that was alarming only to my exaggerated sense of restraint. She discovered roller skating and became an expert skater. She spent every evening at the skating rink while I saw my dream for her future fading and all her 'education' wasted – why did she not study, why did she not seize the opportunity to read, learn? I said little about this to her, for I realized the dreams were mine, and I remembered feeling the same way about Myrtle.

At night, however, when we tugged the bedclothes our way, the extra vicious tug I made towards my side said something of my disappointment in Isabel.

With Isabel at Four Garden Terrace, life had 'episodes'. There was the 'time of the chocolates'. I had peeped, once, into the small front sitting room where the blinds were always drawn and seen, propped around the picture rail, an unbroken row of large chocolate boxes decorated with satin ribbon and printed with English and Highland scenes, and winsome photos of animals. When I told Isabel about the chocolate boxes, she said, one day when Aunty Isy was out, 'Let's explore the front room.'

Just inside the door stood a tall chest with drawers full of clothing and photos. In the bottom drawer we found a set of white knitted baby clothes wrapped in tissue paper; there were baby blankets, too, and nappies. We knew that Dad's sisters Polly and Isy had stillborn babies or those who did not survive beyond a few days or weeks, and we'd had a stillborn brother, and even as children we had sensed a kind of hunger in Aunty Polly's and Aunty Isy's feeling towards us, particularly Aunty Isy's interest in Myrtle, and Aunty Polly's voiced desire to 'adopt' Chicks or June. We quickly shut the drawer and turned our attention to the chocolate boxes. We noted that the cellophane seal appeared to be unbroken.

'She can't have kept them all those years,' we said. We knew Aunty Isy had won the chocolates for her Highland Dancing.

'Let's look inside them,' Isabel suggested.

'Oh no, we couldn't.'

'We'll open one and test it.'

As eager as Isabel to explore the chocolate boxes but aware of the responsibilities of an older sister, I was yet happy to use language to conceal the moral problem.

'Yes, let's test them.' After all, testing was different. If the boxes did contain chocolates *testing* would not be *eating*.

We dislodged one box from the picture rail, and carefully untied the ribbon and slipped off the cellophane cover and wedged the upper half from the lower and looked inside at rows of chocolates in their brown pleated cases.

We sat on the sofa and began to taste.

'They're good, not musty at all.'

We continued to eat, and when we had finished the box, we scattered the paper cases inside, shut the box, returned it to its cellophane cover, and retied the satin ribbon in a bow across the front. We climbed up and set the box on the picture rail.

During our stay at Garden Terrace we ate gradually all the chocolates from all the boxes around the picture rail, returning the boxes when we had finished, and each time we sneaked into the darkened front room we remembered the new baby clothes but did not look at them again, and as we ate our fill, we wondered about Aunty Isy and how her life had been and I told Isabel about Uncle George in bed, and the lanoline, and when we scattered the empty paper cases into the empty box we both felt distaste at what we were doing, eating Aunty Isy's cherished souvenirs: eating, eating. The frill around the paper cases was like the frill, withered at the edges, of those small shells you prise open on the beach, to find a small dead heap with a black dead eye lying inside.

It was at the end of the second term that the explosion came. Isabel finally wrote home complaining that Aunty Isy had starved me for a whole year and that we were both starving and during that winter we were freezing in one bed in a tiny room. Isabel's letter prompted a swift reply from mother to Aunty Isy who then wrote to Dad, her brother, expressing the opinion that 'Lottie has always been a bad manager.' Mother's indignant reply was followed by Aunty Isy's accusation that she had been mistaken in thinking Isabel and I were 'lovely girls'. We had eaten all her souvenir chocolates! Apparently on a rare visit to the front room she found a stray chocolate case on the carpet.

In the exchange of letters, Uncle George's sisters found disparaging things to say about the 'awful Frames', how the children had always been out of control, running wild on the Oamaru hills, how the Frame home was like a pigsty, mother didn't know the first thing about housekeeping. The bitter correspondence continued between Dad and Aunty Isy (mother refused to 'lower herself' by writing after her first two letters), with Dad now using Mum's formal name, Lottie.

The result was that Isabel and I moved from Number Four Garden Terrace, I with shame and embarrassment and a sense of loss in being no longer thought of as a 'lovely girl, no trouble at all', and Isabel with triumph because we had asserted our 'rights', Isabel happily, sociably going to live among friends in a boarding-house whose landlady was well known and liked by a succession of students, I to the only other place available, Stuart House, a hostel where I rented a 'cubicle' for the rest of the year – a narrow space in a large room where each bed was screened by a fibreboard wall about six feet high; and I found little solitude or privacy for studying, reading and writing – and sleeping.

I knew during the first weeks of Isabel's stay in Dunedin that she was lost from me, and I felt sad to lose her: after all, she had been Emily,

No coward soul is mine,
No trembler in the world's storm-troubled sphere.

I think her separation from me was accomplished in those evenings when she skated spinning round and round the rink almost as if unwinding an anchoring thread from her body. She spent hours swimming, coming home to Garden Terrace with her blonde hair green-tinged from the chlorine in the water, and when she opened the door of our room I would always see, behind the face of the student who had been swimming, the face of the child coming home from the baths the day Myrtle was drowned.

The shift from Garden Terrace almost completed our separation. If we saw each other at Training College we said hello in an embarrassed way. And when the letter came from home we met each other briefly to talk about the awful news: 56 Eden Street which we'd rented all those years of our growing up had been sold and the new owner, soon to be married, had given us notice to move out at the end of the year.

Shortly after that the warden of the College sent for me, and when I wonderingly arrived for the interview, she began, 'I want to talk to you about your sister Isabel.'

Isabel, she said, was making a guy of herself both by her behaviour and by the clothes she wore, in particular a skirt printed with a giraffe.

'Fancy wearing a skirt with a giraffe printed on it!' the warden said.

I murmured something sympathetic towards Isabel. Her clothes never shocked us; they were interesting, original. Knowing how many hours we Frame girls had spent trying to sew our own clothes, fitting petersham, making hems even, matching that awkward scoop at the arm of a sleeve to ensure the right sleeve was in the right arm, I thought Isabel's appliquéd giraffe was a triumph of dressmaking. The truth was that no-one else had a skirt with a

42

giraffe on it, therefore Isabel was condemned for her difference. The force of 'no-one else' was a familiar feature of our lives.

'You as her elder sister, are responsible for her,' the warden said, 'Try to influence her not to be so . . . so . . . outlandish.'

I, demure in my ordinary print dress and cardigan, said, as one grownup to another, 'She's very young,' adding, as if I knew the reason for Isabel's behaviour (why should not Isabel have suffered the misery of being in the Sixth Form?), 'she came to Training College too early.'

Then, alarmed, indignant, unhappy, I murmured something about 'conditions at home'. There was sickness, I said, bursting into tears. 'And we're being turned out of our house and we have to find somewhere before Christmas.'

'Well,' the warden said, 'see what you can do to influence your younger sister.'

I said nothing to Isabel about my interview with the warden. I was angry with the concern over a mere giraffe, and now, so many years later, the episode seems unbelievable and wryly amusing but it does show the degree of conformity expected of us. I was ashamed, too, of bursting into tears, although later I hoped the episode had enhanced my poetic role – 'illness in her family – perhaps drink? – turned out of her home . . . a fitting source for a poet . . . what a tragic life . . .'

A few weeks later the warden again 'sent for' me, this time to congratulate me on the children's story I had written and to ask me if I had thought of 'taking up' writing for children. My work showed promise and imagination, she said, while I listened calmly, inwardly disdainful of devoting my life to anything but writing poetry, cherishing the idea of myself as a poet. At the end of the interview the warden said, 'Our little talk seems to have had an effect on your sister; she's much more subdued now and no longer wears that skirt with the giraffe on it.' I didn't explain that the giraffe had become dislodged and Isabel was hoping to sew it when she had 'time'. I knew that her time was taken up with Steve, her boyfriend, tall, handsome, blond, who had a friend Morrie, tall, handsome, dark and very shy, and on one of our meetings to talk about the 'search for a house', Isabel suggested I 'leave all that study' and come dancing with her and Steve, with Morrie as my partner. I rashly agreed and spent an unfamiliar but vaguely exciting evening being partnered by Morrie who divided his time between dancing (and saying very little), and standing with me watching the dancing while he shuffled and hopped, doing a kind of private jig, and sang under his breath,

> Missed the Saturday dance
> got as far as the door,
> couldn't bear it without you,
> don't get around much any more . . .

adding repeats of a chorus, 'Don't get around, don't get around, don't get around much any more,' in his Southland drawl. I enjoyed the otherness of his presence beside me but we were both too shy and when we glanced at each other his face was a dusky red and mine, I know, had its self-conscious blush.

The warden's remarks about my writing encouraged me to think of entering the College poetry competition at the end of the year, to show her and others that I was *really* a poet. In the meantime, I had so much to do and think about and worry about that my only places of peace were the University English lectures where I lived within Shakespeare and Old English, and the reference room at the Dunedin Public Library where I read modern poetry, James Frazer, Jung and Freud. I hadn't even begun to write my 'Growth of Cities', a subject which excited me by its possibilities and repelled me by the prospect that I might have to record boring geographical and historical detail. As a result of cultivating what I thought of as a 'poetic spirit' I had become impatient with everything I decided was 'boring detail', either because I gave it little value in my ideal poetic world or because it reminded me that I was not as clever as I wanted to be and I was growing aware of, and refusing to accept the limitations of my mind. I couldn't even write the kind of poetry that was printed in *Critic*. Who did I think I was, to imagine I'd be a poet?

Faced with 'The Growth of Cities', I felt myself to be a miserable failure. My only hope was to write (and illustrate) the long essay in my own way, that is to attach my own giraffe to the ordinary accepted garb of prose. In the end the text became a geographical and historical and social version of *The Waves*, with bizarre illustrations cut from magazines, as I had not a 'flair' for drawing. I learned later that the verdict on my 'Growth of Cities' was similar to the verdict on Isabel's clothing, although I also learned that someone suggested there might be 'more in me than they knew.'

There were two main delights for me in that final year of College: the discovery of art in the inspiring lectures given by Gordon Tovey, and the performance of the College Choir where all sang, even those without musical voices. We sang 'The Lady of Shalott', 'At Flores in the Azores (the Ballad of Richard Grenville)', and the 'Hymn to Joy' from Beethoven's Ninth Symphony, under the tuition of George Wilkinson, known as Wilkie. I remember rehearsing and rehearsing, and finally singing, full of tears at the momentous occasion, surrounded by singing voices, all in a sensation of being in an upper storey of the mind and heart, knowing a joy that I never wanted to end, and even now when I remember that evening in the Dunedin Town Hall, the massed choir and the massed audience, and people whom one never dreamed would be singing, and I too, singing

> soft and sweet through ether ringing
> sounds and harmonies of joy.

I remember the happiness and recognize it as one of the rewards of alliance with any great work of art, as if ordinary people were suddenly called upon to see the point of view of angels.

The year was ending. I sent my poems to the College Magazine and won the ten shilling first prize for 'Cat'.

> Deaf to the hammering window
> and the idiot boy's mewing
> I leave the torn mice to flow
> through his vacant eyes
> and sit propped up by a fat thinking.
> But the will of the beating boy
> burgles me ear, creeps
> like a curled cat in my brain, purrs and sleeps
> and pads me from the house

to the scratched clouds and the clawed moon;
and the winds like torn mice
flow through my vacant eyes.

The other poem, also printed, was 'Tunnel Beach'.

Perennial of seagull, rooted in sea,
dug in green ache, the seagull bush
draws pleading enough to feed
the dead ears of the cliff with crying
or stuff interminably the world's eyes with tears.

Here in the tunnel, severed from aching, the seagull bush
strangles our groping throat in a white rush of blossom,
acknowledges no roots
in the green guillotine and the seawoman crying hush.

Only where light leaks, where stone people,
slabbing the beach call, call dungeon for their heart's house,
as butchers' bargains, secret Spartan boys,
there the stone minds, the mad minds break
rooting the sea and the white bird
in one bush infinite and alone.

I quote the poems because they, being of the time, speak of my
George Barker-Dylan Thomas influences, and of my struggle to
accept and be responsible for myself as a whole being without
having to conceal my inner dreams in order to preserve them, or
without having to deceive by playing roles of teacher, smiling,
happy, 'a lovely girl, no trouble at all.'

Some memories have been diluted, mostly by the storms that
followed or were given; the colour of those memories has been
washed away, their shape is gone. I knew the family was desperate
to find somewhere to live. Dad, who handled all the money, took
shares in a newly-formed Building Society with the hope of getting
a loan from the monthly ballot, while mother who never had
personal money, contributed her faith, 'God knows what you have
need of even before you ask,' and, miraculously, the following
ballot produced a loan of three hundred pounds, just enough to
buy a ramshackle rat-ridden old cottage set in three and a half
acres of land on the outskirts of Oamaru, just beyond the Gardens

and the Motor Camp. The shift and the search must have been so worrying to me that I don't remember it. When College ended for the year, I went with the Bradleys and Rona Pinder to Stewart Island where we stayed in a cabin on the beach. My memory of that time is contained only in the few snapshots of us prancing on the beach in our home-made sunsuits, of food cooking over a fire tended by two young men, of the interior of our hut with myself in bed, the bedclothes up to my neck, while one of the young men washes the dishes of the night before when we'd had our 'beer party', the symbol then of complete adulthood.

I returned to Oamaru to find that we had shifted house from 56 Eden Street to the old cottage in the grounds known as Willowglen.

6
Willowglen

Willowglen had belonged in turn to derelict families, seldom talked of singly, only as the 'awful D's' or 'those X's' whose children at school were barefooted and ragged and sometimes sick and, growing up, became the makers of social mistakes, the outcasts. During the Depression they had been the real poor, existing on beef and pork bones and specked fruit, getting their clothes in sugarbags from the 'relief depôt'. If you needed to go to the depôt, you were at the end of the world; people said you were stupid and a waste of time and you'd never learn and you infected others. I used to be fascinated by the word *depôt*, with that tiny hat, like a duncecap, above the o, which I later learned was a circumflex, sign of a lost 's'; I imagined the ravines in the landscape of words where the lost letters had fallen.

The house had been empty since the M's left town. The three acres had been planted early in the century by a landscape gardener, with English trees – five oaks, species of pine including a huge northern pine with draped branches which we called the 'ghost tree'; yew and cypress; an orchard of apple, cherry, quince, plum trees; a big pear tree leaning over the roof at the back; masses of spring flowers – daffodils, matchheads, crocuses, along the banks of the creek that flowed through the property. Along the driveway, council property giving us a right of way, there was a plantation of young pine trees. Willowglen was surrounded on three sides by paddocks of matagouri, of swamp, and on one side there was the railway line leading south out of Oamaru.

I remember my stranded feeling of desolation when I walked through the lean-to that was set against the hill at the back of the house and littered with tides of last year's flow of pear-tree leaves, and saw the kitchen with its floor partly of earth, for most of the old wooden floor had collapsed. The kitchen had a coal range and in the larger scullery adjoining there was an old electric range. A tap leading from the rusted water tank outside jutted through the scullery wall. Surprisingly, beyond the scullery there was a small bathroom with a bath and handbasin but no hot water, and, until the tank could be repaired or town water laid on, there was no water. The house had four rooms and the kitchen, scullery and bathroom, and in two of the rooms there were back-to-back fireplaces long disused, filled with crumbling debris from the chimney; and every room had its heap of borer gold dust constantly increased as each human footstep on the rotted floors sent its vibration to the borer-riddled ceiling.

Outside beside the huge magpie-filled macrocarpa tree there was a decayed wash-house with a copper in one corner for boiling clothes washed in the wooden wash-tubs. Along the path from the lean-to, the 'dunny' beside the cypress tree, and soon known as 'the cypress', was covered with the small fragrant white roses known to us as 'dunny roses', and was without a door, while the dunny seat, long and wide like a beach dunny, was set over a deep hole half-filled with old 'kiki' (our word for faeces) in varying shades of brown, topped with faded pieces of newspaper, the *Oamaru Mail* and the *Otago Daily Times*.

The family told me how Isabel and June had scrubbed the house, how they'd helped carry some of the furniture up the steep path but how most of it had to be left 'down on the flat' in one of the two old stables and farm sheds. Bruddie and Dad, their differences temporarily forgotten, worked together planning a water supply, a septic tank and restoring the roof. Mother, overjoyed at her first use of an electric range, set about baking pikelets and scones and rock cakes and rissoles, or, using an electric iron for the first time, she ironed Dad's workshirts and handkerchiefs, and said wistfully, 'If only we'd had these when the kiddies were little!' We girls also enjoyed using the electric iron, after our years of heating the old flat irons on the stove and, sometimes forgetting to wipe the soot from underneath, branding our school uniforms and blouses with black marks that could not be rubbed out; and how swiftly we could now press hems and pleats!

In spite of our ramshackle place we were already at home, or *they* were, for I'd missed the process of moving, and my arrival was like joining the family when the death and the shock of death and the burial were over. Already Dad had begun his routine of heaving 'spare' coal from the engine as he drove the train slowly around the curve by the Gardens and up the steep grade towards Maheno, and the others had learned to scramble with a sack through the wire fence by the wattle tree, among the clumps of wild sweet pea, to collect the precious lumps of railway coal, either 'bright' coal – Kaitangata, or 'dull' coal – Southland lignite. And already the hastily repaired henhouse had been stocked with a dozen White Leghorns, partly to justify the rusty grinder found in the old shed and make it work at grinding oyster shells for the hens' grit. The decrepit cowshed, roofless, with a broken bail, stood waiting at the foot of the hill by the apple shed.

Seeing the earth floor and the 'nowhereness' of the interior of the house, I felt depressed and lonely and I knew the Willowglen house would never be my home; it was too small, everyone was too close to everyone else; in the front bedroom you could hear the wireless from the kitchen as if you were in the kitchen. You could hear the arguments, too, the raised voices, and the soft murmur of pleading that you knew to be, 'Don't raise your voices to each other,' from mother. My sisters and brother and I were now of an age when our lives held an 'inner room' not revealed to one another, although we still talked cheerfully of our dreams, and saw, with much laughter, the 'funny side' of everything. Indeed, that summer we made of the new owner of 56 Eden Street a fictional 'baddie', telling one another stories about him and his certain fate, adding him to our list of villains – Miss Low, the Health Inspector, the MP who didn't answer our request for money to buy clothes, all of whom had been carefully enclosed, rendered powerless, by our web of spoken words.

We gave to the land at Willowglen the kind of love we had not given to 56 Eden Street, although every leaf and plant and insect and the earth itself and the arrangement of buildings and trees had served us nobly. Willowglen was the first home we had owned. Of course the Building Society had to be paid back, and the Starr-Bowkett booklet with its stamped receipts had a place of pride on our new mantelpiece beside Dad's tin of sixpences – a cocoa tin with a slit in the lid where he dropped all his sixpences until the tin was full after which he cut strips of time-sheets, marshalled the sixpences into a long roll, and wrapped them carefully before taking them downtown to be changed into 'real' money.

How we dreamed that summer! Perhaps if we had shifted to Willowglen during the winter we might not have been able to dream our dreams, but it was summer, Christmas just past and we had our own holly tree and for the first time in our lives, our own pine branches instead of macrocarpa – what did we care that we now had no usable fireplace? The mass of blossoms borne by the orchard, the daffodils in their withered tops just showing in the long grass, the luxury of so many trees and so much grass, of swamphens and ducks and eels and water-lilies in the creek, of so much summer sky, and 'down on the flat' a plantation of young pines to listen to with the wind blowing, all gave such delight that we fell in love with the 'outside' at Willowglen. During those marvellous green and gold summer days I found a place by the creek, an old log, like the old birch log of years ago. I sat for hours watching the water, the ducks, the swamphens, and, through the broken-down wire fence, the sheep nibbling the grass in the paddock of half-swamp and half-matagouri, *my matagouri*. My sisters and I explored the roads into town and beyond, and the Old Mill Road which had been part of our childhood and adolescent folklore when to 'live away out past the Old Mill' meant to live as far away as, on the other side of town, 'past the Boys' High', and when to 'go 'round the Old Mill' with a boy meant what you'd expect it to mean.

And when the first autumn dews appeared on the grass, on the days of late January, we picked mushrooms by our own pine plantation and on the hill opposite where you could look down through the gum trees at the Robertson's farm. They had the town milk supply. They had a son Norman going to University with a

Scholarship. I'd spoken to him once or twice. I remember thinking wistfully that perhaps he and I might fall in love and marry.

When Dad was home he too had his place. His end of the table was that near the coal range where he could see through the small window if there were visitors coming up the path, and where he had light to read by. The sofa against the wall just inside the kitchen door was Bruddie's place; his rifle for shooting rabbits hung on the wall above, and in moments of family tension Bruddie would reach for his rifle and begin to clean it, slowly, deliberately, while mother watched anxiously, and Dad, his lips pressed angrily together, smoothed the time-sheets before him on the table or reached for his cocoa tin and began to count his sixpences. Or he'd say, 'Where's my chalk, Mum?'

For years Dad had had stomach pains and because he suspected he might have cancer he refused to go to a doctor; instead, he drank a medicine suggested by Aunty Polly or Aunty Isy, and known as 'chalk'.

And Mum would find the chalk, prepare the dose, and give it to him.

And the episode would be over until the next time.

Like each of us, mother had her dreams of Willowglen. Within her prison of toil, self-imposed (for we felt ourselves to be grown up and were willing to help, partly to erase our now uncomfortable memories of mother's role as an everlasting servant), mother looked out at her dream-place, near in reality, but seemingly removed from her in her prison. She dreamed of when she would go 'down on the flat', 'in the cool of the evening' and just sit, perhaps picnic, under the pine trees and listen to the wind in the trees. Willowglen, we discovered, had a special share of sun. Unlike at 56 Eden Street where the land lay full under the sun and the sky, the house at Willowglen set against a western hill and facing an eastern hill, with the north boundary of hawthorn hedge, may trees, willow trees, had only brief sun in the morning, making the house cool even in summer, but if you looked from the cool and often cold world of the house you'd see, down on the flat by the creek and beyond it, a world where the sun stayed late, in summer until the evening; and perhaps if you looked out, as mother did, when the day and working energy were fast being spent, you might feel 'down on the flat' to be an unattainable world of sun.

When I pleaded for mother to come down on the flat in the sun she said in the tone she used for talking of publication, the Second Coming, and, now, the white fox fur as a twenty-first birthday present, 'One of these days.'

She added, inserting the biblical language that made the 'flat' seem more distant and dream-like, 'One of these days "in the cool of the evening" I'll come and sit under the pine trees in the sun.'

Word came in January that I was to teach Standard Two at Arthur Street School, Dunedin. I had applied for a class of that age living in what we had learned was 'the latent period' when children were thought to be malleable, responsible, untroubled, or if there were 'trouble' it was secret, unrealized – oh how thoroughly we thought we knew that mythical 'child'!

And in response to my advertisement in the *Otago Daily Times*, 'Quiet student seeks board near Arthur Street School', I heard from a Mrs T in Drivers Road, Maori Hill, offering me 'full board'. And so once again Isabel and I travelled south by the familiar slow train to Dunedin, Isabel to her second year at Training College and to Mrs R in Union Street where she'd stayed since we left Aunty Isy's, and I to the house of Mrs T in Maori Hill and my year as a probationary teacher at Arthur Street School.

7
1945: One

When as children we experimented with our identity and place by
moving from ourselves to encircle the planets, in our repeated
inscriptions – name, street, town – Oamaru, North Otago, Otago,
South Island, New Zealand, the Southern Hemisphere, the World,
the Universe, the Planets and Stars, we were making a simple
journey in words and, perhaps, a prophecy of being; we were lyric
poets forced to realize the possibility of epics, and in a matter-of-
fact way we included these epic possibilities in our ordinary
thinking. I mention this because 1945, a year that began for me as
a personal lyric, ended through accident of circumstance, of
national and world events, as an epic embracing the universe, the
planets and the stars, this time expressed in deeds, not in words.

I arrived with my growing self in Dunedin. This was to be the
year of my twenty-first birthday at the end of August. 'Twenty-
firsts' as they were known, were part of the continuing ritual of
growing up, when one became 'of age', a legal citizen able to vote,
to make a will, or, as the song said,

> I'm twenty-one today.
> I've got the key of the door,
> I've never been twenty-one before.
> I'm twenty-one today.

At the end of the year, also, I hoped I would gain my Certificate
as a teacher, after my probationary year at Arthur Street School. I
hoped also to add another unit to my arts degree course, and as I
felt that English III would prove to be too engulfing of my interest,
I decided upon Psychology I, a first year of Psychology.

My secret desire to be a poet, fed by the publication in the

54

College Magazine of my two poems ('Now they'll find out that I'm really a poet!') occupied much of my planning. I was as anxious to impress with my imagination as I had been during my years at school, only here there were so many more people each with so much more imagination, prose writers and poets everywhere, for I was learning to get copies of *Critic* by lingering with apparent casualness around the entrance to the University near the *Critic* 'bin' with its enticement, 'Take One'. Contributions still needed a visit to the office where the poem or story could be placed. I don't know why I didn't post a contribution. I suspect that I was ignorant and innocent in most human activities, including posting letters. I was still not aware of the number of everyday chores dealt with by ordinary people. Based on my life at home, my supposition was that letters were written only to other towns with news of events such as births, deaths, marriages, or past or future travel, while telegrams were mostly a swift form of communicating the fact of death or the time of arrival of a train 'passing through' or depositing relations; and parcels meant Christmas. I had scarcely begun to study the primer of adult living. I knew of joy and of love discovered at the point of loss, and I had accepted death. I felt that I could see the feelings of people beneath their faces, in their eyes, their imposed or swift unguarded expressions, and in the words they spoke. The War still haunted and confused me – 'the pity of war, the pity war distilled', and it was the poets who continued to illuminate for me the places no-one else seemed to want to talk about or visit. I thought often, with longing, of the prophecy, 'Nation shall not lift up sword against nation, neither shall they learn war any more.'

I boarded with Mrs T, a widow with a married daughter, Kathleen, living in the new government housing estate at Wakari, where Mrs T spent most of her days, taking the bus after breakfast – 'I'm going over to Kathleen's' – and coming home at about the same time I came home from school. Mrs T's only topic of conversation was 'Kathleen, Bob and the children', what they did, what they said, how they felt, with much of her thoughts occupied by what she would give them for presents. 'I saw something in Arthur Barnetts and I said to myself, "That will be just right for

Kathleen's youngest, Kathleen has been looking everywhere for something like that." ' Bob worked in the Electricity Department, the showroom in Princes Street, and could get heaters at a discount.

For the sake of appearances I sometimes had meals with Mrs T instead of taking them to my room 'as I have study to catch up with and lessons to mark and prepare . . .' and then I would sit opposite her and listen, fascinated, while she described the day 'over at Kathleen's' – how they'd done the washing together and tidied the house, how Kathleen and Bob were hoping some day to get carpet 'edge to edge' in every room. 'There are quite a few carpeted now edge to edge.' I, the 'quiet shy teacher, no trouble, no trouble at all,' spent most of my free time in my room marking, preparing lessons, and cutting out paper stars in different colours to reward the children's efforts; and studying my textbook of Psychology; and writing and reading poems.

Mrs T's house was like Jessie C's house in Oamaru – a place where 'other people' lived; with carpets and wallpaper printed with roses, with plenty of furniture and knick-knacks, and upholstered sofas without a tear; and throughout the house, no sign of furniture's stuffing or wooden floor or scrim behind the wallpaper. There was comfort with an air of concealment. Brought up in a house where we always knew and in many cases could see what happened behind the walls and beneath the floor, I never felt quite at home in the houses of 'other people'. Even at Willowglen, the desolation of having an earth floor gave a sense of reality (so strong it became unreality) that felt more a part of living than the padded secrecy of houses like Mrs T's.

I delighted in the children at school and in teaching. I was full of ideas for encouraging individual development. I revelled in the children's art and in their poetry, for they wrote poetry and stories almost every day, and these, with the paintings, I pinned around the walls for everyone to enjoy. I took pains, too, in teaching other subjects. My failure was as a member of the staff, for my timidity among people, especially among those who might be asked to judge and comment on my performance as a teacher, led to my spending my free time alone. Too timid to go to morning and afternoon tea with a room full of other teachers, I made excuses about 'having work to do in the classroom', aware that I was going against all the instructions about the need to 'mix in adult company, take part in social events and discussions with other teachers and parents', and that 'morning tea in the teachers' room' was an almost sacred ritual. My fear of being 'inspected' by the headmaster or inspector inspired me to devise a means of postponing the day of reckoning, by inventing a serial story which I could continue whenever I heard the steps of authority approaching along the corridor, so that a visit by the headmaster to a class sitting rapt with attention (the content of the story ensured a rapt audience), might 'prove' my ability as a teacher with the result that I would 'pass' my 'C' Certificate at the end of the year.

My escape from teaching was the Psychology class and the Psychology laboratory where we performed a range of interesting experiments and tests supervised by two fresh young lecturers, Peter Prince and John Forrest whom we called Mr Prince and Mr Forrest, but whom I nicknamed HRH and Ash (after Ashley, the fair young man in *Gone with the Wind*, played by Leslie Howard). As these two young men – recent graduates, in a world where young men were few – were in a sense for public and student consumption, they became the object of rumour, speculation and fantasy. I preferred HRH because, unlike Ash, he appeared to be an 'introvert', and according to the magical fixed classification of people, 'introverts' were the artists, the poets. I'd see HRH, his face turned towards the sky, his pipe in his mouth, striding with his long-legged springing gait, down Frederick Street towards the University, and I'd think, 'He's in another world.' He blushed easily, too, and like my admired G. M. Cameron he had an endearing awkwardness of speech and gesture. Ash, not so tall, was handsome, fairhaired with a lock of hair draped over his forehead, and unlike HRH who wore dark suits, Ash wore a rust-coloured sports coat and tomato-red socks which he actually referred to one day in the laboratory, saying, 'How do you like my tomayto socks?' pronouncing tomato the *American* way.

Some of the women swooned over Ash.

It was Ash – Mr Forrest – who arranged for gramophone recitals to be held regularly in the gramophone room of the Music Department.

'All those records and few people hearing them,' he said in his forthright way. (He was becoming known for his 'forthrightness' and for his unconventional clothing.)

One day when I decided to go to the recital and I was standing outside the door of the gramophone room trying to pluck up courage to go in, I heard the piano being played. I opened the door and peeped in and there was Mr Forrest playing the piano. He stopped at once and prepared the records for the recital. But I had heard him playing the piano, up and down the keys in a flourish and swoop like a concert pianist, marshalling the notes together in a travelling force going somewhere, and not simply picking out notes into a 'tune', separating them and giving them no say in the whole music. Apart from the loved Schubert songs and the 'tunes' of Walt Disney's *Fantasia*, and the new songs we had learned at Training College, including old carols

> I think this child will come to be
> Some sort of workman such as we
> So he shall have my goods and chattels,
> My planks of wood, my plane, my drill,
> My hammer that so merry rattles . . .

and

> Little Jesus sweetly sleep do not stir
> We will lend a coat of fur . . .

I still had little knowledge of classical music, and I had never listened to a long piece of music – a symphony or concerto. That day, Mr Forrest played a record of Tchaikovsky's *Symphony Pathétique*, and among the handful of students, I listened to the unaccustomed sounds dragging, dragging their awful burden of gloom, on and on, and when the music arrived at the 'tune' I knew as

> This is the story of a starry night
> The faded glory of a starry night . . .

I experienced the delight of recognition. I listened to the end, in love with the music and its churning sadness, and Tchaikovsky became (after Schubert) my favourite composer.

'I suppose you all know César Franck,' Mr Forrest said.

The audience looked as if they knew César Franck.

'We'll play César Franck next time,' Mr Forrest said, pronouncing the name with such assurance and familiarity.

The music room became another place where I felt at home and where I learned to listen to music that lasted more than three or five minutes. Why had I not known before that listening to a symphony was like reading a book in all its progressions, with its special shape, and silent and noisy moments? I learned to say, carelessly, 'Adagio – did you like the *Adagio*? That *Andante* passage . . .' I began to go to lunch-hour piano recitals in the Town Hall and although at first I clapped in the wrong places, thinking the music was ended, I soon learned the pattern. I talked, too, as people talked who regularly went to music recitals and symphony concerts, 'Oh, smell the mothballs in the fur coats! They only listen to music once a year. Just imagine, once a year! And all that coughing, right in the middle of that slow movement, they didn't even cough in the places where they thought it was fair to sneak in a cough or a cleared throat!'

And one day John Forrest startled me into a new perception of him by saying suddenly, in the music room, 'But Shubert is my favourite composer.'

Schubert! *To Music. Thou holy art in many hours of sadness.*

In spite of the worries about teaching and my future, I found the year mostly pleasurable. At school and University I gave little thought to my home and family, and when I spent one of my few weekends at home, I tried to detach myself from the place and the people. My family appeared like tired ghosts trying to come to life for the occasion; both mother and Dad were still pursued by *toil*, and the extra weariness now lay in the long walk up the hill, Dad with his home-made leather work-bag crammed with railway coal, mother, during the day when no-one was home, carrying the groceries which the boy from the Self Help or the Star Stores had delivered to the shed. Coming home for the weekend I'd always find that mother had bought a jar of coffee, that dark sweet liquid with the splurp taste, known as Gregg's Coffee and Chicory where the outside of the bottle became sticky with the spilled syrup. Drinking coffee was a sign of being grown up; therefore I drank coffee. Also, one of the lecturers at University had spoken to me using the name, *Janet*, when I had always been known as *Jean*; therefore I was now officially *Janet*. During the weekend, Dad would bring a pile of Sexton Blake library books for me to read, and I'd race through the exploits of Sexton Blake and Tinker so that I could talk about them with him. The attentive habits of my parents saddened, pleased, and infuriated me, leaving me with a feeling of helplessness – what could I do for them? I could see the pattern of their past lives slowly emerging, like a script written with invisible ink and now being made visible to me, warmed by the fire kindled simply by my growing up. I could see, too, an illumination produced by that same fire, the shadows emerging as recognized shapes of a language full of meaning for me: the language of the love and loss and joy and torture of having a place fast within a family when all my awakening longing was directed towards being uprooted, quickly, without leaving behind a cluster of nerve endings, broken threads in danger of being renewed.

The year was half gone. My personal lyric began its silent terrifying progression towards the planets and the stars. At the beginning of the month when I was to celebrate my twenty-first birthday, my coming of age, the War was suddenly over, having pursued me through all the years of my official adolescence, as part of the development of my body and mind, almost as an ingredient of my blood, leaving its trace everywhere, even in my hair and my (picked or bitten) fingernails. There was the usual spring snowfall that year, killing the newborn lambs but letting the early crocuses survive. Everyone rejoiced that the War had ended, and it was enough to rejoice and not notice or think about the fact that the atom bomb had been born, it also given its own life and responsibility. My coming of age was lit by the mushroom fire that made shadows of all those caught in its brightness; a spectacular illumination of the ceremonies of death, 'ashes to ashes, dust to dust.'

On 28 August I 'came of age' without a party but with some special presents given to me by my family – 'things' showing that I was a part of the world, after all: I had a new wristlet watch, and a new pair of plaid pompommed slippers with fleecy lining.

That month, as a kind of surface skimming of all the feeling set to boil away until old age, I wrote and published my first story, 'University Entrance' for which the *Listener* paid two guineas.

And now the year was passing quickly with the school inspector's crucial final visit soon to be faced. Inevitably, one bright morning of daffodils and flowering currant and a shine on the leaves of the bush along Queen's Drive where I walked to school each morning, of a hint of warm gold in the sharp lemon-coloured sunlight, I arrived at school to find that it was the Day of Inspection, and at midmorning the inspector and the headmaster came to my class-room. I greeted them amiably in my practised teacherly fashion, standing at the side of the room near the display of paintings while the inspector talked to the class before he settled down to watch my performance as a teacher. I waited. Then I said to the inspector, 'Will you excuse me a moment please?'

'Certainly, Miss Frame.'

I walked out of the room and out of the school, knowing I would never return.

8
1945: Two

At first, drunk with the sense of freedom, all worry gone, I simply enjoyed the sparkle of the morning. Then, reality, taking over, directed my route down London Street, the street of doctors, and I chose a doctor's rooms near the foot of the hill, and walked in to consult a Dr William Brown, as harmless and anonymous a name as I could find. I explained to Dr Brown that I was very tired and felt I needed a rest of a few weeks. 'I'm in my first year teaching,' I said, bursting into tears.

Dr Brown obligingly gave me a certificate for the headmaster, to explain my temporary absence.

After posting the certificate in the box at the corner, I began three weeks of pure freedom. I went to University classes, to music recitals. I read and wrote. 'I have three weeks' leave,' I told my landlady who, absorbed in her family, at once began to talk of when Bob would be given his annual holiday. Kathleen and the children so much wanted to go to Queenstown.

'I have so much work to do,' I said, 'that you probably won't see much of me, for meals and so on, and I'll leave a note in plenty of time if I'm not going to be in to dinner.'

'You're so thoughtful,' Mrs T said. 'I'm lucky to have such a quiet student. You wouldn't even know you were in the house, you're so quiet!'

(A lovely girl, no trouble at all.)

At the end of my third week when school again loomed before me I was forced to realize that suicide was my only escape. I had woven so carefully, with such close texture, my visible layer of 'no trouble at all, a quiet student, always ready with a smile (if the decayed teeth could be hidden), always happy', that even I could not break the thread of the material of my deceit. I felt completely isolated. I knew no-one to confide in, to get advice from; and there was nowhere I could go. What, *in all the world*, could I do to earn my living and still live as myself, as I knew myself to be. Temporary masks, I knew, had their place; everyone was wearing them, they were the human rage; but not masks cemented in place until the wearer could not breathe and was eventually suffocated.

On Saturday evening I tidied my room, arranged my possessions, and swallowing a packet of aspros, I lay down in bed to die, certain that I would die. My desperation was extreme.

The next morning, near noon, I woke with a roaring in my ears and my nose bleeding. My first thought was not even a thought, it was a feeling of wonder and delight and thankfulness that I was alive. I staggered from my bed and looked at myself in the mirror; my face was a dusky red. I began to vomit, again and again. At last my nose stopped bleeding but the roaring in my ears continued. I returned to bed and slept, waking at about ten o'clock that evening. My head still throbbed, my ears rang. I hurried to the bathroom, turned on the tap, and vomited again. Mrs T who had spent the weekend at Kathleen's and had been home about two hours, came to the door of her bedroom.

'Is everything alright?' she asked.

'Oh yes,' I called. 'Everything's fine. I've had a busy day.' (No trouble, no trouble at all.)

'Kathleen and Bob are in the midst of it all,' Mrs T said, not explaining but evidently pleased. 'In the midst of it all.' We said goodnight and I went to my room and slept.

The next morning, the dreaded Monday, I woke with only a slight headache.

'My leave has been extended,' I told Mrs T 'I have research to do.' I was now so overjoyed that I was alive when my intention had been to die, that school seemed a minor problem. I explained to the headmaster, possibly over the telephone and later by writing, that I had been advised to give up teaching. I did not say that it was I who was giving myself this advice.

I found a job washing dishes in the student canteen. I tried to turn hopefully towards my future. I felt that I would never again choose to kill myself.

It happened that part of our Psychology course was the writing of a condensed autobiography. When I finished writing mine I wondered whether I should mention my attempt at suicide. I had now recovered; in a way, I was now rather proud for I could not understand how I had been so daring. I wrote at the end of my autobiography, 'Perhaps I should mention a recent attempt at suicide . . .' describing what I had done but, to make the attempt more impressive, using the chemical term for aspirin – *acetylsalicylic acid*.

At the end of the class that week, John Forrest said to me, 'I enjoyed your autobiography. All the others were so formal and serious but yours was so natural. You have a talent for writing.'

I smiled within myself in a superior fashion. Talent for writing, indeed. Writing was going to be my profession!

'Oh I do write,' I said. 'I had a story in the *Listener* . . .'

He was impressed. Everyone had been impressed, saying, 'The *Listener*'s hard to get into.'

John Forrest looked at me closely. 'You must have had trouble swallowing all those aspros?'

'Oh, I drank them with water,' I said calmly.

That evening as I was preparing to go to bed, Mrs T answering a knock on the door called to me, 'There are three men to see you. From the University.'

I went to the door and there were Mr Forrest, Mr Prince and the Head of the Department who spoke first.

'Mr Forrest tells me you haven't been feeling very well. We thought you might like to have a little rest.'

'I'm fine thank you.' (No trouble, no trouble at all.)

'We thought you might like to come with us down to the hospital – the Dunedin hospital – just for a few days' rest.'

I felt suddenly free of all worry, cared for. I could think of nothing more desirable than lying in bed sheltered and warm, away from teaching and trying to earn money, and even away from Mrs T and her comfortable home; and away from my family and my worry over them; and from my increasing sense of isolation in a brave bright world of brave bright people; away from the War and being twenty-one and responsible; only not away from my decaying teeth.

'John will come to visit you,' the Head of the Department said.

John! The use of first names, common among the young lecturers and their students but still a novelty to me, pleased and alarmed me. 'That's kind of you, Mr Forrest,' I said primly.

And so I was admitted to the Dunedin hospital, to Colquhoun Ward which, I was soon shocked to find, was a *psychiatric ward*.

The doctors, Marples and Woodhouse, two young house surgeons, were questioning and kind. The nurse, Maitland Brown, a member of the Evangelical Union training to be a church missionary, talked to me of her hopes and dreams. I remember only one other patient in the bed next to mine, a strange woman who'd had an operation and kept denying it. I, brought up in a film star world of instant judgement on the looks of people, thought her repulsive and ugly with her red face, coarse skin, her small eyes with their ginger lashes and her thinning ginger hair. The dislike of her was general. I wonder now about the treatment of psychiatric and other patients who release, as if it were a chemical, an invitation to be disliked and who therefore have to fight (inducing further dislike and antagonism) for sympathy and fairness. When one day two ambulance men arrived to take the ugly patient to 'another hospital', I learned that the 'other hospital' was *Seacliff*. Seacliff, up the main trunk line, the hospital of grey stone, built like a castle. Seacliff where the loonies went. 'You won't be going there, of course,' Maitland said. 'There's nothing wrong with you.'

And after my three weeks in hospital for observation, that was indeed the verdict. Mother was asked to travel to Dunedin to take me home, and after a holiday at home I'd be good as new, they said.

Faced suddenly with the prospect of going home, I felt all the worries of the world returning, all the sadness of home and the everlasting toil of my parents and the weekly payments on the blankets and the new eiderdown from Calder Mackays, and the payments to the Starr-Bowkett Building Society or we'd be turned out of our house again; and the arguments at home, and mother's eternal peacemaker intervention; and my decaying teeth; and my inability to find a place in the Is-Land that existed by absorbing, faster and faster, each tomorrow. If only I had the world of poetry, openly, unashamedly, without having to hide it in secrecy within myself!

In my state of alarm about my future, when I saw mother standing there at the entrance to the ward, in her pitifully 'best' clothes, her navy costume and her navy straw hat with the bunch of artificial flowers at the brim; with a hint of fear in her eyes (for, after all, I had been in a 'mental' ward) and her face transparently trying to adopt the expression *All is well*, I knew that home was the last place I wanted to be. I screamed at mother to go away. She left, murmuring her bewilderment, 'But she's such a happy person, she's always been such a happy person.'

I supposed, then, that I'd stay in hospital a few more days then be discharged, find a job in Dunedin, continue my University studies, renouncing teaching for ever. I did not realize that the alternative to going home was committal to Seacliff. No-one thought to ask me why I had screamed at my mother, no-one asked me what my plans were for the future. I became an instant third person, or even personless, as in the official note made about my mother's visit (reported to me many years later), 'Refused to leave hospital.'

I was taken (third-person people are also thrust into the passive mood) to Seacliff in a car that held two girls from Borstal and the police matron, Miss Churchill. Miss Churchill! How curiously events and people and places and names moved between fiction and fact!

9
1945: Three

Writing an autobiography, usually thought of as a looking back, can just as well be a looking *across* or *through*, with the passing of time giving an X-ray quality to the eye. Also, time past is not time gone, it is time accumulated with the host resembling the character in the fairytale who was joined along the route by more and more characters none of whom could be separated from one another or from the host, with some stuck so fast that their presence caused physical pain. Add to the characters all the events, thoughts, feelings, and there is a mass of time, now a sticky mess, now a jewel bigger than the planets and the stars.

If I look through 1945 I see the skeleton of the year and shadowing it with both the shadow of death and of life, the atom bomb, the homely crocuses surviving in the late spring snow, birthdays and death-days, and two or three other events bringing those dreamed-of planets and stars within the personal world of myself and many others in New Zealand. The events were the publication of *Beyond the Palisade*, poems by a young student at the University, James K. Baxter, *A Book of New Zealand Verse* edited by Allen Curnow, and a collection of stories edited by Frank Sargeson, *Speaking for Ourselves*. As a child I had looked on New Zealand literature as the province of my mother, and when I longed for my surroundings – the hill, the pine plantations, 56 Eden Street, Oamaru, the foreshore and the sea to waken to imaginative life, all I could do was populate them with characters and dreams from the poetic world of another hemisphere and with my own imaginings. There was such a creation as New Zealand literature; I chose to ignore it, and indeed was scarcely aware of it. Few people spoke of it, as if it were a shameful disease. Only in the Modern Bookshop in Moray Place were there shelves of slim New Zealand books from small presses, and I had even bought some, and tried and failed to write poems like those in the books. James Baxter's poems with their worldwide assurance also intimidated me. The anthologies, however, were different: their force and variety gave me hope for my own writing while wakening in me an awareness of New Zealand as a place of writers who understood how I had felt when I imported J. C. Squire to describe my beloved South Island rivers, and though I read the poem again and again I had to be content with the Congo, Nile, Colorado, Niger, Indus, Zambesi: beautiful names but those of another world.

But here, in the anthology of New Zealand verse (they were still not brave enough to call it *poetry*) I could read in Allen Curnow's poems about Canterbury and the plains, about 'dust and distance', about our land having its share of time and not having to borrow from a northern Shakespearian wallet. I could read, too, about the past, and absences, and objects which only we could experience, and substances haunting in their unique influence on our lives: the poem 'Wild Iron' reads to me like part of a history of New Zealand and its people.

And there was Denis Glover using the names of our own rivers and places, and even writing about the magpies, perfectly recording their cries on a misty autumn morning. Each poet spoke in his and her own way and place, and there was Charles Brasch confiding in the sea as I had confided, without words, in the Clutha, 'Speak for us, great sea.'

The stories, too, overwhelmed me by the fact of their belonging. It was almost a feeling of having been an orphan who discovers that her parents are alive and living in the most desirable home – pages of prose and poetry.

Time confers privileges of arrangement and rearrangement undreamed of until it becomes Time Past. I have been writing of the memory of publication of stories and poems. In actual memory I am sitting talking to two Borstal girls, on the way to Seacliff Hospital where I shall be a committed patient.

10
1945: Four

The six weeks I spent at Seacliff Hospital in a world I'd never known among people whose existences I never thought possible, became for me a concentrated course in the horrors of insanity and the dwelling-place of those judged insane, separating me for ever from the former acceptable realities and assurances of everyday life. From my first moment there I knew that I could not turn back to my usual life or forget what I saw at Seacliff. I felt as if my life were overturned by this sudden division of people into 'ordinary' people in the street, and these 'secret' people whom few had seen or talked to but whom many spoke of with derision, laughter, fear. I saw people with their eyes staring like the eyes of hurricanes surrounded here by whirling unseen and unheard commotion contrasting strangely with the stillness. I grew to know and like my fellow patients. I was impressed and saddened by their – our – capacity to learn and adhere to and often relish the spoken and unspoken rules of institutional life, by the pride in the daily routine, shown by patients who had been in hospital for many years. There was a personal, geographical, even linguistic exclusiveness in this community of the insane who yet had no legal or personal external identity – no clothes of their own to wear, no handbags, purses, no possessions but a temporary bed to sleep in with a locker beside it, and a room to sit in and stare, called the *dayroom*. Many patients confined in other wards of Seacliff had no name, only a nickname, no past, no future, only an imprisoned Now, an eternal Is-Land without its accompanying horizons, foot or handhold, and even without its everchanging sky.

In my book *Faces in the Water* I have described in detail the surroundings and events in the several mental hospitals I experienced during the eight following years. I have also written factually of my own treatment and my thoughts about it. The fiction of the book lies in the portrayal of the central character, based on my life but given largely fictional thoughts and feelings, to create a picture of the sickness I saw around me. When one day a fellow patient, seeing workmen outside digging drains, said to me, 'Look, they are digging our graves,' I knew she believed this. Her words are an example of the words and behaviour I used to portray Istina Mavet. Even in my six weeks' stay I learned, as if I had entered a foreign land, much of the language and behaviour of the inhabitants of the land. Others also learned fast – the girls from Borstal were adept at livening their day by a 'performance' based on example.

My previous community had been my family. In *To the Is-Land* I constantly use the first person plural – we, not I. My time as a student was an I-time. Now, as a Seacliff patient, I was again part of a group, yet more deeply alone, not even a creviced 'I'. I became 'she', one of 'them'.

When I left Seacliff in December 1945, for a six-month probationary period, to return to a Willowglen summer, the shiningest time at Willowglen, I felt that I carried within me a momentous change brought about by my experience of being in a mental hospital. I looked at my family and I knew that they did not know what I had seen, that in different places throughout the country there were men and women and children locked, hidden away with nothing left but a nickname, with even the word *nick*name hinting at the presence of devils. I noticed that the behaviour of my family had changed in subtle ways related to my having been a patient in Seacliff where the loonies lived. Why do I use once again the metaphor with a spider? It seemed as if, having been in hospital, I had, like a spider, woven about me numerous threads which invisibly reached all those who 'knew' and bound them to a paralysis of fixed poses and expressions and feelings that made me unhappy and lonely but gave me also a recognition of the power of having spun the web and the powerlessness of those trapped within it.

When I'd been home a week or two my family grew less

apprehensive in my presence – the change showed in the lessening of fear in their eyes; who knows what I might do; I was a loony, wasn't I? Mother, characteristically, began to deny everything. I was a happy person, she said. There must have been some mistake. I found that everyone was pleased when I treated the matter as a joke, talking of amusing incidents at the 'country estate', likening it to a hotel. I described the surroundings. 'It's like a whole village,' I said. 'They have their own farm, their own cattle and pigs, and all the waste from the food goes into the pig tin. They have their vegetable garden, and their flowers, too. And the grounds are full of trees, and there's a magnolia tree near where the Superintendent lives.'

It was easier to talk as if I were a child describing what I had seen and what adventures I'd had on my holiday.

I didn't tell them how I had peeped through the fence of a building called *Simla*, away upon the hill, where there were strange men in striped shirts and trousers and some without trousers, walking round and round in a paddock with the grass worn away; and how I'd seen a paddock of women, too, wearing the dark blue striped clothes; and how there was a cart, like a rickshaw, that passed every day by the ward, how it was full of coal and two men harnessed to the cart carried the coal, driven by one of the attendants; how, curious as ever, I had peered into a room that stank of urine and was full of children lying in cots, strange children, some of them babies, making strange noises; their faces wet with tears and snot; and I didn't say how there was a special section for the patients with tuberculosis, and how their dishes were boiled in a kerosene tin on the dining room fire, and the nurses spent some time in the small linen cupboard folding the cardboard to make the daily supply of boxes, like strawberry boxes, for the TB patients to spit in.

After Christmas it was suggested that perhaps a holiday would be 'good' for me, and so June and I set out for two weeks in Picton, mother's old home town, where we spent the usual summer sandfly-bitten time travelling around the Sounds in launches, meeting relatives, hearing new details of family history, while I, strongly under the influence of my past year of listening to music, composed in my mind what I called my Picton Symphony in Green and Blue. My memory of the holiday is scattered – like seeds, I imagine, a handful eaten by summer-visiting birds migrating from winter memories, or by native birds that feed time-long on the memory, others not surviving, others grown into plants that cannot be recognized or named. I know that I took home the memory of those steep green oppressive hills, their bushclad slopes rising as inescapably close as neighbours.

Asked to describe the holiday, June and I told the family what we knew they wanted to hear, to try to make everyone happy. We had grown up, you see, in a thorough school, in this with our mother as teacher. And once again I began to prepare for another year in Dunedin.

I planned to find a 'live-in' job, and to 'take' Philosophy II, Logic and Ethics, but sit no examinations. I had been assured that although I sat no end-of-year Psychology examinations I would be granted a pass based on my year's work. Perhaps I neglected to fill in the correct forms: I discovered that I had been marked *Failed*. Failed!

In the meantime, at home, there was the problem of having my life savings of twenty pounds returned from the Public Trust Office who had taken charge of my affairs as I was officially insane. Once again my sisters and my brother and I 'banded together' to try to assert our rights, with Isabel composing an earnest letter to the Public Trust Officer who replied that his confiscation of my 'property' was in my own interests as I was officially insane and would not have legal rights until my 'probation' period of six months had ended, and then only if the doctor declared my sanity.

Perhaps, then, I could be given a sickness benefit until I began working again?

My visit to the Seacliff doctor at the Oamaru hospital brought its own bewilderment, for the medical certificate stated: Nature of Illness; *Schizophrenia*.

At home I announced, half with pride, half with fear, 'I've got *Shizzofreenier*.'

I searched through my Psychology book, the chapter on Abnormal Psychology, where I found no reference to *Schizophrenia*, only

72

to a mental illness apparently afflicting only young people like myself – *dementia praecox*, described as a gradual deterioration of mind, with no cure. In the notes at the end of the chapter there was an explanation that *dementia praecox* was now known as *schizophrenia. Shizzophreenier.* A gradual deterioration of mind. Of mind and behaviour. What would happen to me? No cure. Gradual deterioration. I suffered from *shizzophreenier.* It seemed to spell my doom, as if I had emerged from a chrysalis, the natural human state, into another kind of creature, and even if there were parts of me that were familiar to human beings, my gradual deterioration would lead me further and further away, and in the end not even my family would know me.

In the last of the shining Willowglen summer these feelings of doom came only briefly as passing clouds block the sun. I knew that I was shy, inclined to be fearful, and even more so after my six weeks of being in hospital and seeing what I had seen around me, that I was absorbed in the world of imagination, but I also knew that I was totally present in the 'real' world and whatever shadow lay over me, lay only in the writing on the medical certificate.

Towards the opening of the University year when I advertised for a live-in job in Dunedin, describing myself as a 'research student', I received a reply from Mrs B, of Playfair Street, Caversham, who kept a boardinghouse and cared for elderly women. I was to be a housemaid-waitress-nurse, with three pounds a week 'all found', and afternoons free. Afternoons free. Time to write my stories and poems.

11

The Boardinghouse and the New World

Once again I travelled south by the slow Sunday train to Dunedin, stopping at every station, looking out from the old-fashioned carriage, tacked on for the few passengers, at the spiralling links of tarpaulin-covered trucks. As usual there were unloadings, loadings, jolts as the trucks were removed, long periods when the carriage at the end seemed to stand alone in the midst of paddocks of gum trees, tussock, manuka scrub, *matagouri*, swamp, sheep, derelict houses, as if it made an excursion into a nowhere that was also a yesterday, filled with peace and sadness. I looked out of the old-fashioned push-up window (as opposed to the newer wind-up windows of the express trains) and I felt a force that could only have been the force of love drawing me towards the land where no-one appeared to be home. I felt a new sense of responsibility to everything and everyone because every moment I carried the memory of the people I had seen in Seacliff, and this knowing even changed the landscape and my feeling towards it.

When the train stopped at Seacliff Station I saw the few *parole* patients waiting on the platform to watch the train go by. I *knew*, you see. Inwardly I kept describing myself in the words that I knew relatives and friends now used, 'She's been in Seacliff. They had to take her to Seacliff.' And I thought of the horror in mother's voice when, years ago, the doctor had suggested that Bruddie should go there, and mother had replied, 'Never. Never. No child of mine will ever go to that place.' But I was a child of hers, wasn't I? Wasn't I? And she had signed papers to send me there. I felt uneasy, trying to divide out portions of family love to discover how much was mine.

I looked around the carriage at the 'ordinary people'. Did they know where I had been? If they knew, would they look at me and then turn away quickly to hide the fear and fascinated curiosity as if they were tasting an experience which – thank God, they thought – they would never know but about which they wondered furiously, fearfully? If they knew about me, would they try to find a sign, as I had done when I, too, used to stare at the 'loonies' on Seacliff Station.

Well, I thought, the signs were often secret but I knew them now, I was an experienced observer, I had visited the foreign land.

Also, I remembered with dread, they say I have *shizzofreenier*. A disease without hope.

The wheels of the train, however, which all my railway life had said Kaitangata, Kaitangata, Kaitangata, remained uninfluenced by my strange disease: their iron on iron said, obstinately, *Kaitangata, Kaitangata, Kaitangata.*

The train arrived at Dunedin Station. I felt quite alone, as if I belonged nowhere. All those marvellously belonging days at Training College when we sang 'The Deacon went Down', and talked knowledgeably of Party, and crit lessons, and days of control; the English and French lectures, the year of teaching children I had grown to love, had vanished as if they had never been, an impression deepened by the fact that since my disappearance to Seacliff there'd been no word from College or school or University, except a letter from my friend Sheila and a note from John Forrest to invite me to have 'little talks' with him during the coming year. I clung to the idea of having someone to talk to, and relished the bonus that the someone was an interesting young man.

I was taking my new status seriously. If the world of the mad were the world where I now officially belonged (lifelong disease, no cure, no hope) then I would use it to survive, I would excel in it. I sensed that it did not exclude my being a poet. It was therefore with a feeling of loneliness but with a new self-possession, unlike my first fearful arrival in the big city of Dunedin, that I took a taxi to Playfair Street, Caversham, in the heart of the country of the Industrial School.

South Dunedin – Kensington, Caversham, St Kilda – was a poor community where lives were spent in the eternal 'toil' with the low-lying landscape reflecting the lives, as if effort and hope were here washed away in the recurring floods while the dwellers on the hill suburbs prospered. I had taught in Caversham school and at Kensington in the school 'under the railway bridge', and I had seen the poverty, the rows of decaying houses washed biscuit-colour by time and the rain and the floods; and the pale children lank-haired, damp-looking, as if they emerged each day from the tide.

My memory of the boarders and the landlord and landlady and their child is momentary, like a hastily sketched scene in black and white giving only the outline of each person with the hair growing like grass out of their skull. They still hold, however, an invisible bowl brimful of feeling, and it is their feeling unspoken and spoken, that I remember most vividly. They were unhappy anxious people trying desperately to pretend they were happy, and seizing occasions of joy to recount, each to the others, at mealtimes, as a way of contributing to the possibility of happiness. The men usually were employed at the Railway Workshops, the women in the factories – the chocolate or jam factory – or a branch of the woollen mill. One young man lost his job every few weeks, found another, lost that, and at night, at dinner, the others talked about his success or failure, explaining, excusing, condemning. They criticized each other, poked fun, pounced swiftly on the unconforming. I remember the landlady's husband only as a tall pale stooped man who carried firewood from the shed into the sitting room where everyone gathered in the evening, the women with their knitting, the men with playing cards or their sporting newspapers; and sometimes one of the boarders who was acknowledged to have 'failed' in life (as opposed to the others who still had valid excuses and reasons), a thin woman in her middle thirties, without a husband or lover (the basis for her being judged a failure) played the yellowing keys of the piano while the middle aged bachelor, a salesman, plump, popular ('he's always the same, you know where you are with him') sang the current favourite song,

Beyond the sunset
to blissful morning . . .

From the moment of my arrival I explained that I'd be very busy out of working hours and so would prefer at times to have my meals in my room. I was a student, engaged in private research, I said – I with my ready smile (hoping that I concealed my badly decayed teeth), sympathetic voice, no obvious physical deformities; and my upstanding mass of frizzy ginger hair. My duties were to prepare and serve breakfast, to clean the house, and to attend to the four elderly women who lived, bedridden, each in a corner bed, in the large front room. I washed them, helped to turn them or arrange the rubber ring beneath their gaunt bodies where the skin hung in folds like chicken skin with bumps where feathers might once have been. I rubbed methylated spirits on their bedsores, and powdered their bodies. I fed them, sometimes with the aid of a white china feeding-cup. I helped them use the wooden commode or arranged a bedpan beneath their drooping buttocks.

I was surprised to find that one of the women was old Mrs K, Aunty Han's sister, Aunty Han being the wife of Uncle Bob who, retired from his bakery in Mosgiel, now sat in a tobacconist's 'possie', an enclosure the size of a telephone booth, where he sold cigarettes, tobacco, *Best Bets* and *Sporting News* and Art Union tickets. Old Mrs K, who was also the mother of the student whose name I had 'dropped' as being my 'aunt's niece' when I was accepted for Training College, was a tall woman with large defined bones and an imperious face with pointed nose and chin. The family came from 'up Central', and even Mrs K had absorbed some of the Central Otago hill formation into her own body. Like her sister, Aunty Han, she had a mouth and lips prepared to register instant disapproval. Dad used to say that Aunty Han's mouth was like the behind of an egg-bound hen.

Here at Mrs B's, I became friends with Aunty Han's sister. I found that I had gentleness and everlasting patience with the sick and the old. I enjoyed waiting on people, attending to their comfort, doing as they asked, bringing the food they ordered. I had no impatience, irritation, anger, to subdue: I seemed to be a 'born' servant. The knowledge frightened me: I was behaving as my mother had done all the years I had known her, and I was enjoying my new role: I could erase myself completely and live only through the feelings of others.

My bedroom, once a linen cupboard, was small with shelves along one wall, and a narrow bed against the other wall. The view from the one small window was 'pure Caversham' – dreary grey stone buildings with a glimpse of the tall chimneys of *Parkside*, the home for the aged, resembling my idea of a nineteenth century English workhouse. When I finished my morning's work I'd go to my room and sit on my bed and write my stories and poems, for just as when I had been a child there was a time for writing and the knowledge that other children were writing their poems, now I was aware of writers in my own country. My inspiration for my stories came partly from my reading of William Saroyan, and my unthinking delight, 'I can do that too.' And besides the excitement of being in a land that was coming alive with its own writing, *speaking for itself*, with many of the writers returning from the War, bringing their urgency of experience, I felt the inspiration of my own newly acquired treasure – my stay of six weeks in a mental hospital, what I had felt and seen, and what I had become, my official status of schizophrenia. And while I fed the guests at the boardinghouse, they fed me from that invisible bowl of their feelings.

My life away from the boardinghouse consisted of evening lectures on Logic and Ethics, and weekly 'talks' with John Forrest in a small room on the top storey of the University building known as the Professors' House. I also spent time in the Dunedin Public Library where I read case histories of patients suffering from schizophrenia, with my alarm and sense of doom increasing as I tried to imagine what would happen to me. That the idea of my suffering from schizophrenia seemed to me so unreal, only increased my confusion when I learned that one of the symptoms was 'things seeming unreal'. There was no escape.

My consolation was my 'talks' with John Forrest as he was my link with the world I had known, and because I wanted these 'talks' to continue, I built up a formidable schizophrenic repertoire: I'd lie on the couch, while the young handsome John Forrest, glistening with newly-applied Freud, took note of what I said and did, and suddenly I'd put a glazed look in my eye, as if I were in a dream, and begin to relate a fantasy as if I experienced it as a reality. I'd describe it in detail while John Forrest listened, impressed, serious. Usually I incorporated in the fantasy details of my reading on schizoprenia.

'You are suffering from a loneliness of the inner soul,' John said one day. For all his newness and eagerness to practise psychology and his apparent willingness to believe everything I said, his depth of perception about 'inner loneliness' was a mark of his special ability. He next made the remark which was to direct my behaviour and reason for many years.

'When I think of you,' he said, 'I think of Van Gogh, of Hugo Wolf . . .'

I, in my ignorance, knowing little of either Van Gogh or Hugo Wolf, and once again turning to books for my information, discovered that Hugo Wolf 'd. insane', and that Van Gogh 'shot himself in despair at his condition'. I read that Schumann, too, 'suffered serious deterioration in mental health'. All three were named as *schizophrenic*, with their artistic ability apparently the pearl of their schizophrenia. Great artists, visionaries . . .

My place was set, then, at the terrible feast. I had no illusions about 'greatness' but at least I could endow my work and – when necessary – my life with the mark of my schizophrenia.

When John Forrest learned that I was writing poems and stories, he was delighted. He suggested that as I wrote each I should give it to him to keep, and I, therefore, began to bring him my stories and poems. I kept 'pure schizophrenia' for the poems where it was most at home, and I looked forward to John Forrest's praise of my efforts; and when I had saved enough money to buy a secondhand Barlock 20 typewriter and type my work using, at first, one or two fingers, I felt that I possessed all in the world that I desired – a place to write, time to write, enough money to live on, someone to talk to or at least someone to try to impress, for most of my thoughts I kept to myself, and a disease interesting enough to be my ally in my artistic efforts and to ensure, provided I maintained the correct symptoms, that I had the continued audience of John Forrest. I was playing a game, half in earnest, to win the attention of a likeable young man whose interest was psychology and art; yet in spite of my pretence at hallucinations and visions I was growing increasingly fearful of the likeness between some of my true feelings and those thought of as belonging to sufferers from schizophrenia. I was very shy, within myself. I preferred to write, to explore the world of imagination, rather than to mix with others. I was never withdrawn from the 'real' world, however, although I was convincingly able to 'use' this symptom when the occasion required.

I was not yet aware of sexual feelings although I no doubt experienced them, innocently not recognizing them. Then one day when I was exploring a case history of schizophrenia, I read of a woman who was afraid (as I was, although I also was deterred by lack of money) to visit the dentist, and on exploration in the Freudian manner, it was discovered that *fear of the dentist* was common in those suffering from schizophrenia, *fear of the dentist* being interpreted as *guilt over masturbation* which was said to be one of the causes and a continued symptom of schizophrenia!

I pondered this: I was certainly afraid of visiting the dentist as I knew that my teeth were now beyond repair (the general opinion in New Zealand then was that natural teeth were best removed anyway, it was a kind of colonial squandering, like the needless uprooting of forests). As for masturbation, it was a word of which I was ignorant and an act of which I was innocent. This new fact, however, made me curious enough to investigate both meaning and deed, for surely I must know if it were to be thought one of the causes of my disease! It happened that both my sisters and I, feeling we needed further sex education and having no-one to give it to us in its theory, sent for a widely advertised book which arrived in its plain wrapper: *Meeting and Mating*. Everyone who was *educated*, with a wholesome attitude to sex and marriage, was reading *Meeting and Mating*, and recommending it. We found in it details we had searched for in vain in mother's *Ladies' Handbook of Home Treatment* with its chapter 'God's Great Out-of-Doors' intended to be read by women about to marry. It referred also to masturbation, describing it in detail, explaining how it was acceptable in both men and women with no need for guilt.

And of course I tried it. And childhood was suddenly long long ago, for I *knew*, and I couldn't return to the state of not knowing, and the remaining curiosity was, How might it be if one never knew? A few weeks later I said to John Forrest, 'It's awful, I can't tell you, for years I've been guilty about it. It's . . . it's . . .'

He waited expectantly.

'It's masturbation, worry over masturbation . . .'

'It usually is,' he said, and began to explain, as our book had explained, how it was 'perfectly alright, everyone did it.'

The pattern of that 'little talk' was so perfect that I imagine (now) a fleeting triumph passing over John Forrest's Freud-intensive face: here was a textbook schizophrenic.

I continued to fear that I might once again be left with no-one to talk to, that is, in a 'normal' state of nearness to mental breakdown, for I was on the usual adolescent path of worry and wondering how to 'cope' with everyday living; yet, strangely, in order to lessen my anxiety, I found myself forced to choose a more distinctly signposted path where my journey drew more attention and so, I found, drew more practical help. I don't think it occured to me that people might be willing to help me if I maintained my ordinary timid smiling self. My life so far had trained me to perform, to gain approval by answering questions in examinations, solving problems, exhibiting flashes of 'cleverness' and 'difference'. I was usually ashamed of my clothing. I was baffled by my fuzzy hair and the attention it drew, and the urgency with which people advised that I have it 'straightened', as if it posed a threat. I was not fluent in conversation, nor witty, nor brilliant. I was an ordinary grey-feathered bird that spent its life flashing one or two crimson feathers at the world, adapting the feathers to suit the time of life. In my childhood I had displayed number riddles, memorizing long passages of verse and prose, mathematical answers; now, to *suit* the occasion, I wore my schizophrenic fancy dress.

During 1946, when my 'probationary' period was over, I was declared sane; I felt a twinge of loss, very slight, for I had written a collection of stories and poems which John Forrest had shown to

Denis Glover of the Caxton Press who was interested in publishing the stories in a book, with the poems perhaps following. I felt I had begun my career as a writer.

Then, towards the end of the year, John Forrest announced that he had applied for work as a psychologist in the USA where he hoped to get his PhD. He would be leaving New Zealand early in 1947. He suggested that if I needed someone to talk to, he could recommend his friend in Christchurch, Mrs R, with whom he had spoken about me, he said, adding that she, being of an artistic nature, was interested in my 'case'.

'I'll find a job in Christchurch and perhaps take a course at the Canterbury University,' I said, very calmly as I saw my secure schizophrenic world of 'little talks' beginning to fall apart, leaving me alone in an alien city. I wondered why I had ever thought that I belonged in Dunedin or how I would ever belong in Christchurch. The Caxton Press was in Christchurch, and the book they were planning some time to publish – perhaps the book would be like a relation, living near by, and I'd not be isolated?

I wondered where I would go. I knew I could not stay beyond one or two months at home, without being overtaken by unhappiness at the everlasting struggle of everyone there – for money, or love or power or an ocean of peace. There was always a hotel or boarding-house to give me work, room and board, but why did 1946 need to end?

I stood on the cliff trying to catch at the wings of 1946 as they beat at the salt-strewn earth and grass in preparation for their flight forward into yesterday. In reality, I said goodbye to all at Playfair Street, Caversham – the four old ladies and the boarders with their secret failures and shames and small shared happinesses, and my landlord and landlady and their small child of four who still didn't speak although everyone pretended not to notice; and I left with my brand-new reference should I look for work in Christchurch, 'Polite to the guests at all times, industrious, a pleasure . . .' and a tiny black kitten supposedly male but actually female which I named affectionately, Sigmund, changed later to Sigmunde, known as Siggy; and once again, a railway person

82

bound forever to the dock and the wild sweet peas and 'the rust on the railway lines', I travelled north on the Express and as the train approached Oamaru, before the Gardens, I caught a quick glimpse, looking left, of Willowglen putting on its gloss for the summer.

12

Willowglen Summer

I had not known a complete winter at Willowglen: only June and Bruddie and Mother and Dad had suffered the misery when the creek flooded and the driveway, churned by the cows (how could we have a ready-made cowbyre and three acres of land without cows to share it?) made the track to the gate impassable; I had spent only weekends huddled under blankets, clutching a stone hot-water bottle, in the freezing front bedroom, or, dressed in farm clothing, gumboots and Dad's fishing raincoat, wandering the hills to keep warm.

Dad and Bruddie had worked hard to make improvements to the house. There was no longer an earth floor in the kitchen. The roof was watertight. Pipes (which froze in winter) had been laid, connecting us to town water, and a hot-water cylinder installed in the scullery. We now had a telephone in the passage, a party line, with a long horn-like earpiece, and when the telephone rang it was usually mother who answered it. Dad refused, his fear transparent, while mother, equally fearful, prepared for the shock of what the message might be, for a telephone, like a telegram, was used in urgency, and could mean life or death. The telephone book was always on the 'fernstand' which, like some of the pieces of furniture small enough to fit into the house, had always been part of the family with names that spoke of another age: the 'fernstand' – that never held ferns; Grandad's chess table with its dark burned engravings of a long-dead King and Queen; the *chiffonier* . . .

It was a paradisal summer. I had my place to sit, on the fallen birch log by the creek, where I could watch the pukeko, the ducks and the eels, and look through the sheltering willows to the paddock where the sheep and cattle owned by the stock and station agent were held each week before being driven up the road to the Waiareka Saleyards to be trucked out to the Pukeuri Freezing Works which I knew to be the *Abbatoir*, although for many years I confined the word to a kind of porch of consciousness where words linger and come and go without an investigation of their meaning or an invitation to that lightning room of realization. Sometimes, futilely, I was able to rescue a sheep from the swamp, and for this service, the stock and station agent, a tall man with a square face and horn-rimmed glasses and an appearance that I might have associated with a player of the cello or piano, paid me a fee of five pounds.

From behind the willows I could see, unseen myself, the road and the postman cycling to our letterbox, the last on the street before the farms and their paddocks and the Old Mill Road. I wondered would the postman bring me a letter? From where? From whom? Dad had made a letterbox in the shape of a house, with a chimney and painted doors and windows, red walls and a green roof with eaves, and when the postman had cycled past I'd search the letterbox house. At Christmas, John Forrest sent me a card. I treasured it, trying to work out the degree of affection expressed by 'Yours very sincerely'. Was it more or less than 'Yours sincerely'? With my destructive sense of realism I recognized that there wasn't much hope in 'Yours very sincerely', not even if it were examined letter by letter or repeated softly in a romantic voice. I was not in love with John Forrest, yet I needed his interest and attention and it was satisfying to notice the eagerness in mother's eyes when she asked, 'Have you heard from Mr Forrest?' and to make sure I quelled any hopes she might have by replying, 'It's not like that, mother. I am temporarily transferred to him. It's a known phenomenon. You wouldn't understand.'

It was also a summer of foreboding and change. Isabel, swimming in the baths, had collapsed and just managed to pull herself from the water. The doctor who was called to her said, 'Her heart.' The repetition being too appalling to consider, we put the incident aside; I'm not sure whether we told our parents. Isabel had finished an energetic first year of teaching and she and her devoted boyfriend were considering engagement and marriage.

Isabel and June and I, summer-close after our inevitable grown-up separation, discovering in ourselves a new feeling for our parents and the sacrifices they had made for us, decided that now was the time to share what money we had to give mother the holiday she had dreamed of, a visit to Picton, her home town. Dad showed no interest in going, for he had annual holidays at Aunty Polly's, usually in the football season, for Test Matches. Now mother was to have *her* holiday.

'Oh no,' she said. 'You kiddies use the money.'

We insisted. Mother was naturally fearful after an absence of nearly thirty years.

We persuaded her to go, taking Isabel with her, and all – Dad, Bruddie, June, Isabel and I, contributed to her funds, and in early February, carrying her first class free railway ticket in her new purse, and wearing her best – her only – costume and a new straw hat, mother set off with Isabel for her dreamed-of holiday.

We saw them onto the Express train. In our newly found sensitivity to what we called with sadness, regret and guilt, 'the kind of life mother must have had,' we tried to calm her observed apprehension at the thought of leaving home. We gave instructions that either mother or Isabel should telephone within the first few days of their arrival.

'Just to let us know.'

'And you *are* pleased you're going, aren't you, Mum?'

We knew she was pleased. We could see in her face the surfacing of former pleasure – Oh Waikawa Road, Oh Old Caps and down the pa, Oh the sounds, and Port Underwood, Diffenbach and the Pebble Path, remember the Pebble Path, kiddies, the storms and the shipwrecks. Oh the Pioneers . . .

We waved the train out of honest sight, that is, it disappeared past the engine sheds into pure flat distance where the two railway lines merged as we'd been taught to draw them in our lessons on Perspective, and soon the train and the people in it were a narrow line, an I, with a wisp of smoke, an S, above it, out past the Boys' High and Pukeuri on the way across the Canterbury Plains to Christchurch and Picton.

13

Another Death by Water

Mother's absence was like a death. Dad sat morosely at his end of the table by the coal range reading the latest *Humour*, with no-one to sugar and stir his tea and share his excitement when the bubbles, portents of *parcels*, rose to the surface – Look, two parcels! . . . and no-one to scratch his back and share his bed and complain to – 'Your feet are like lumps of dripping.'

June and I were to prepare the meals and help Bruddie with the cows, but after one day when the household was running smoothly and we'd surrendered to Dad's wishes not to 'cook anything fancy', mother's absence was like black frost in the sunless house. We missed Isabel too, in a different way; we missed her endless preparations for this and that, seeing to clothes, lengthening or shortening hems, trying to mend her shoes, giving her frank opinions on everything and everyone; and imagining what her 'future' would be. She had felt that one year of teaching was enough. She would get married, but apart from that, she might be a journalist on a big newspaper, or – something, surely *something*. When the world overtook her in Dunedin she used to go skating; here in Oamaru she went swimming at the Baths.

On the second afternoon of the Picton holiday, the phone rang, and June answered it, and heard through the static and crackle, that it was 'Picton calling.' Dad was at work, and Bruddie was out. Aunty Grace was calling from Picton. Then there was an invisible commotion in the kitchen, like static leaked from the telephone: Isabel, swimming in Picton Harbour, had collapsed and was drowned. There was to be an inquest, after which Mother would bring Isabel home by train.

There was no use even supposing that there had been a mistake:

Isabel drowned. It was almost ten years since Myrtle's death, and this new blow like a double lightning strike burned away our thinking and feeling – what was there to think about, to feel?

The phone rang again. It was Dad: he'd heard the news and was coming home. Bruddie was coming home too. The news was everywhere: Family tragedy of ten years ago repeated. Oamaru girl drowned.

Some called her 'girl', some called her 'woman'. Isabel May Frame in her twenty-first year.

June and I were still alone in the house consoling each other when someone knocked at the back porch door. It was JB! The headmistress of Waitaki, Miss Wilson, known to Isabel, June and me as 'the magnificent Titanic, the mighty modern ship, fifteen thousand tons of steel . . .' I think the amazement of receiving a visit from the headmistress of Waitaki, after all those years at school in a vital separation of home life and school life, almost overlaid our shock. Miss Wilson actually sat on *our sofa*, our sofa with all its exposed springs and stuffing and the dark patch near the armrest, still mapping the place where, years ago, Bruddie's tomcat had peed, and where we'd tried to remove the stain and the smell with our Christmas bottle of carnation scent.

And suddenly Miss Wilson was putting her arms around us and we were all crying, and we thought, If only Isabel could see us, with JB!

My momentary feelings about Isabel's death, as with Myrtle's, that a problem may have been solved but at too great a cost, were overtaken by the dreamlike reality of the first death by water, and the fact that I chose to identify both in a quote from T. S. Eliot, reminding me that I still inhabited a literary world. I had lived through The Waste Land; I had met Phlebas the Phoenician, who,

> a fortnight dead,
> forgot the cry of gulls.

I had known and experienced the rhythm and feeling of Virginia Woolf's Waves, the tragedy of Tess and Jude and the blow after blow struck at the Brontë family. This new death came as an epilogue to the old stories and a prologue to the new, in our own land where the 'great sea' and the rivers would speak for us and we would 'speak for ourselves', where even now, Time had at last taken up residence, on the Canterbury Plains – not too far from Picton – as

> . . . the nor'-west air nosing among the pines
> . . . the water-race and the rust on the railway lines

even those railway lines merging in the distance to a thin perspective that became the dark shaft of absence.

Once again our grief and tears fitted into the familiar pattern, as the ordinary objects became the most poignant: the unfinished sewing, the undone hems of summer dresses, Isabel's new 'jiffy' coat, a short coat with wide sleeves in fashion at the time, the white summer shoes lying in the middle of the bedroom where they'd been dropped the day she left for her holiday. There was the added tragedy of mother's holiday and the fictional perfection of the events with no account taken of fairness or unfairness. Mother's burden was unthinkable: the drowning, the inquest (her second inquest), and the long train journey home with what was now officially 'the body'.

We waited on the platform of the Oamaru station for the train from Picton. Everyone knew, and looked at Dad, Bruddie, June and me, with sympathy. Towards the end of the platform at the goods entrance by the men's lavatories, the funeral director waited with his hearse backed to the platform. The bookstall and tearooms were open for the Express, and the waitresses were standing behind the counter in a line, ready for the rush of passengers for their hot pies, sandwiches, cakes and soft drinks. Perhaps everyone didn't know – there were tides of knowing and not knowing surging back and forth as new passengers, strangers, arrived, and waited; and beyond the platform, past the rows of old red carriages and trucks, the calm summer sea, stony grey-green, gently floated fringes of waves among the rocks along the foreshore. I could not see the water but I knew it and even in my mind I could touch the bubbles of foam and feel the water like a grey-green stone suddenly transparent and flowing.

We heard the telephone ring in the loco foreman's office, and I thought, That's Pukeuri ringing, the train's on its way. I didn't know if my surmise was correct, I knew only that just before the arrival of every train, the telephone rang in the loco foreman's office: that was railway *lore*.

There was a rush of smoke and steam and the sound of brakes and everyone stepped back from the platform to avoid being 'sucked under' – another response to railway tradition. And then there was the funeral director with his hearse as near to the train as he could back it, and they were lifting out of the goods van a coffin coloured dull silver, only it was lead.

'To stop her from smelling,' someone whispered, but I can't remember who said it, for such a remark, inconsiderate then, could have been made only by Isabel herself!

And there was mother coming down the steps of the carriage; hugging and tears, and few words, Dad's, 'the arrangements have been made,' and our 'Miss Wilson from Waitaki came to see us,' said with a kind of glee as if death had prompted us to begin a long accounting: loss and profit, the first bonus.

Mother was bewildered, her eyes were frightened and her hair beneath the 'picture hat' of straw had turned from brown-grey to white.

Willowglen, unlike 56 Eden Street, Oamaru, with its big, dark, apple-smelling front room, had no place to accommodate the dead; besides the hill was too far and too steep for a coffin to be carried, and so Isabel remained at the undertaker's chapel and was buried from there, and only Bruddie and Dad and mother attended the funeral. Perhaps some of my memories of that time were there, too, and were buried with Isabel.

The letters and telegrams of sympathy came and were answered. The undertaker's itemized bill came and was paid. There was a doctor's bill, addressed to Isabel, 'for attendance at swimming baths', for the time she collapsed. And among the letters of sympathy was one from John Forrest: beginning, 'I am deeply grieved to learn of the shocking bereavement you and your family have sustained' and ending, 'Yours very sincerely, John Forrest.' I remember the complete letter for the shock of its language and my inability to accept the formal conventional expressions of sympathy and to accept that John Forrest was so lacking in imaginative understanding that he could write such a letter. I felt betrayed by my own adopted world of language. What reached me was not a message of sympathy but language which I, harshly critical, and making no allowance for the difficulty of writing such letters, condemned as the worst example of prose. Where were the personal, friendly words of the young man who said I suffered from a 'loneliness of the inner soul'?

I was not to know that John Forrest was putting language to good use: he was trying to escape from the several women students who had formed romantic attachments to him!

Death is a dramatic accomplishment of absence; language may be almost as effective. I felt that both Isabel and John Forrest had vanished.

We each bore our grief alone, for Isabel had shared with each, different aspects of her growing up. For many years it was 'Dots and Chicks' – Isabel and June – the inseparable companions as it had once been 'Myrtle and Bruddie', while I, the middle child, moved from group to group according to my age and interests, and when Bruddie became ill, and Myrtle died, I was alone until Isabel and I composed our group, after which June, growing up, again joined Isabel, while I became alone again. Bruddie, except in his earliest days, was always alone. Yet Isabel had been so full of life that her presence and her opinions were hard to dismiss, and when we began to deal with her 'things' we knew she would be furiously angry to see her best shoes and Jiffy coat and her fitting 'Shazaam' jersey being worn by others. She had once said, 'When I die and you take my clothes and wear them, I'm going to come down and haunt you.' Down? Perhaps she believed in Heaven?

When my eldest sister Myrtle died in her sixteenth year she did not leave parts of herself, her presence, at 56 Eden Street, perhaps because the house never belonged to us and there was always the danger that we could be 'turned out on the street', whereas Isabel, who had loved Willowglen, did not really leave it, and although the house was small there was room for the memory of Isabel both inside and outside among the orchard trees and the pine trees, the silver poplars, the cypress and the five oaks; by the creek and the may tree, the elderberry and the hawthorn hedge; beneath the huge macrocarpa where the magpies lived, and the moreporks and the little owl, known during the war as the 'German owl' because it was said to attack smaller birds; and in the calm golden sunlit grass, 'down on the flat.'

The now familiar ritual of death and burial having been completed, I decided to keep to my plan of living and working in Christchurch. I needed to leave Willowglen. There was an undercurrent of 'I hope it doesn't affect Janet too much. You know ... she's been in Seacliff.' Since my six weeks in Seacliff there was an unwillingness to discuss 'serious' matters with me, a special protectiveness which I disliked. Also, I was timid about meeting people, and when visitors came as they did often during the time of Isabel's funeral, I hurried to my room, pursued by mother who stood in the doorway, bewilderment and reproof in her eyes, 'Why don't you come out?'

Or, if visitors were expected, Mother or Dad would say, 'Mrs W is coming over this afternoon. Is Janet going to come out?'

I was in hiding. I was grieving. I didn't want anyone to 'see', for since I had been in hospital, I had found that people didn't only 'see', they *searched* carefully.

I scanned the Situations Vacant columns of the Christchurch *Press*. The only vacancies with Accommodation were in Children's Homes, the School for the Deaf at Sumner, and the usual hotels and boardinghouses. Studying a map of Christchurch and its suburbs, I grew increasingly alarmed by the length of the streets and the unfamiliar names that were yet familiar – Linwood, Burwood (wasn't there a home for wayward girls, like the industrial school at Caversham?), Burnham with the miles of huts of the military camp; Rolleston, Templeton, Hornby (*Hornby* sharp in the memory because every year at Christmas, Bruddie had asked for a *Hornby train*). I thought of the Christchurch railway station echoing with people and train sounds and the whoosh of the steam; trains from everywhere, on different tracks, people asleep leaning on white pillows against the carriage window with the beads of water running down the pane; people wiping the steam with their sleeve, to look out, sleepily, at the yellow lights of the refreshment rooms and the ledge along the outside with the litter of other trains – the empty blue-ringed railway cups and saucers with their dregs of railway tea and soggy crusts of ham sandwiches and ends of cigarettes, De Reszke or Ardath . . .

I found on the map the street where the Caxton Press had my stories to publish. They were printing one in the new magazine, *Landfall*, under the name *Jan Godfrey*, the name being chosen to honour my parents – Jan because Dad called me Jan, and Godfrey, because Godfrey was mother's maiden name. I found also the suburb where Mrs R, John Forrest's friend, lived. And there was the University – dare I go near it? I found it impossible to equate all my dreams with what appeared to be a formidable unyielding reality.

After receiving an application form from the School for the Deaf, and feeling that they wanted to know 'too much about me', I answered an advertisement for a housemaid-waitress at a small hotel in the city, quoting my reference, 'well-spoken, polite to the guests at all times. Honest, industrious . . .' and found myself hired by the proprietor of the 'racing' hotel, the Occidental.

My early acquaintance with words and their significance comes to mind now. I *decided*. I had a *destination*.

Once again I set out on a train journey, north across the Canterbury Plains to Christchurch.

14

Dear Educated

Loss, death, I was philosophical about everthing: I still had my writing, didn't I, and if necessary I could use my schizophrenia to survive. I enjoyed working at the hotel, learning the language of horse racing, of trainers, breeders, buyers, owners, who were the main clientele, and I found the routine satisfying – serving meals on time and bar lunch at five in the evening, and seizing the opportunity to speak French to the French buyers, and feeling slightly superior when they asked why I, with 'my education' worked as a waitress, and giving the usual reply because I was not yet able or ready to call myself a 'writer', 'I'm engaged in private research.'

After work, alone in my room, I saw my tiny triumphs of self-esteem fading as I angled the duchesse mirror, to contemplate the horror of my decayed teeth. There was no escape from them; they ached; my entire face throbbed. I snuggled under the bedclothes with a hot-water bottle pressed upon my jaw. I knew I'd be forced to act very soon. I knew that the public hospital would fill or extract teeth free, but how could I ever think of being brave enough to make an appointment? And all the time I was aware of a dreadful feeling of nothingness which was somehow intensified by the city itself – the endless flat straight streets, the sky without a horizon of hills, the distant horizon without sea. I felt as if I and the city were at the bottom of a huge well walled with sky, and who could climb the sky? When people came to their front or back doors to look out, where did they gaze? I felt so lonely without even the hills close by, like human bodies, for comfort.

After a few weeks in Christchurch I arranged an appointment with Mrs R, John Forrest's friend, with the intention of asking her to help me with arrangements for having my teeth extracted and come with me to the dental department of the Public Hospital but when I presented myself at her house in an exclusive suburb and she, a tall angular woman dressed in fawn and brown, opened the door, I, sensing the impossibility of being able to explain my plight, I, standing there (mouth closed), a blooming young woman of twenty-two with no obvious disabilities, again turned on my 'schizophrenia' at full flow: it had become my only way of arousing interest in those whose help I believed that I needed. Nevertheless, it was several weeks before I could say that my urgent problem was my decaying teeth. Mrs R kindly arranged for me to have my teeth extracted at the Public Hospital; she would come with me, she said, and might it not be a good idea for me to admit myself as a voluntary boarder to Sunnyside Mental Hospital where there was a new electric treatment, which, in her opinion, would help me. I therefore signed the necessary papers.

I woke toothless and was admitted to Sunnyside Hospital and I was given the new electric treatment, and suddenly my life was thrown out of focus. I could not remember. I was terrified. I behaved as others around me behaved. I who had learned the language, spoke and acted that language. I felt utterly alone. There was no-one to talk to. As in other mental hospitals, you were locked up, you did as you were told or else, and that was that. My shame at my toothlessness, my burning sense of loss and grief, my aloneness, and now, with another sister, June, soon to be lost in a marriage, I felt as if there were no place on earth for me. I wanted to leave Sunnyside, but where could I go? I grieved for everything lost – my career as a teacher, my past, my home where I knew I could never stay more than a few weeks, my sisters, my friends, my teeth, that is, myself as a person. All I had left was my desire to be a writer, to explore thoughts and images which were frowned on as being bizarre, and my ambition thought to be suspect, perhaps a delusion. My only writing was in letters to my sister and parents and brother, and these were always censored, and sometimes not mailed: I remember one instance of a letter written to my sister June where I was actually quoting from Virginia Woolf, in describing the gorse as having a 'peanut-buttery smell'. This description was questioned by the doctor who read the letters, and judged to be an example of my 'schizophrenia'. For I was now officially suffering from schizophrenia, although I had had no conversation with the doctors, or tests. I had woven myself into a trap, remembering that a trap is also a refuge.

And when I had been in hospital several months beyond the voluntary period and was declared a committed patient, that was the beginning of the years in hospital which I have already described, setting out only, as I have said, the actual events and people and places, but not myself, except for my feeling of panic simply at being locked up by those who reminded me constantly that I was 'there for life', and as the years passed and the diagnosis remained with no-one apparently questioning it even by formal interviewing or tests, I felt hopelessness at my plight. I inhabited a territory of loneliness which I think resembles that place where the dying spend their time before death and from where those who do return living to the world, bring inevitably a unique point of view that is a nightmare, a treasure, and a lifelong possession; at times I think it must be the best view in the world, ranging even farther than the view from the mountains of love, equal in its rapture and chilling exposure, there in the neighbourhood of the ancient gods and goddesses. The very act of returning to the world, however, tends to remove that view to the storeroom of the mind described by Thomas Beecham as 'the room two inches behind the eyes.' One remembers the treasure and the Midas effect of it upon each moment, and sometimes one can see the glitter among the ordinary waste of each day.

The years that followed, until 1954 when I was finally discharged from hospital, were full of fear and unhappiness, mostly caused by my confinement and treatment in hospital. Early in my stay there were two or three periods of several weeks when I was allowed to leave hospital and each time I needed to return as there was nowhere else for me to live; I was fearful always, like a condemned person returning to the executioner.

During my first return to Oamaru I advertised in the Situations Wanted column of the *Oamaru Mail*, signing myself, 'Educated', and from the three replies, all of which began, 'Dear Educated', I selected one from Mr O whose wife was bedridden; suffering from what used to be called 'creeping paralysis'. For a month I cleaned their house, washed and ironed, attended to Mrs O who lay quietly immersed in the squalor of illness while her husband, even in his health and his absence all day at his work, bore the traces of his wife's immersion: he sweated into his white neatly ironed shirts, and there was always sweat on his forehead. They did not speak much to me except to note their physical conditions.

'My husband sweats a lot,' Mrs O said.

'The doctor says her condition is gradual,' Mr O said.

After waking with delight in the Willowglen surroundings, and walking in the crisp air through the wet grass, as if in a bath of sun and green and blue, taking the short cut through the Oamaru Gardens by the glittering pond noisy with ducks, up across the railway line to the lower part of the South Hill, and stopping briefly to look out over the town and the sea, all drenched with morning; and going up the O's path past the grannys' bonnets to the front door, I'd enter this house of grey people washed with sweat and tears, and I'd feel the gentle flow of sunlight and morning drained away. There was not even a view from Mrs O's bedroom. A great dark wardrobe, placed half in front of the window, cast a steep shadow shaped like a warrior with arm raised to destroy.

I left the O's. My wages gave me enough money to buy a set of upper teeth. I decided to accept the invitation of my sister and her husband to stay a while at their Auckland home.

In Auckland I was in a state of sensitivity to everything around me – the strangeness and heat, the everlasting sound of the cicadas and crickets, the bite of the mosquitoes, my first experience of the subtropical light alternating between harsh brilliance and paradisal cloud-softness, like a storm oppressively, perpetually brewing. It was nearing summer, and the world was filled with blue flowers that attracted the blue of the sky, almost drinking it in until at evening their colour darkened with the excess of blue. I experienced a feeling of nowhereness and nothingness as if I had never existed, or, if I had, I was now erased from the earth. I had somehow fallen into a crevice in time; and many of these feelings were a result of my being 'in touch' with no-one, and of having no-one to talk to from within. I was my usual smiling self, smiling, flashing my bulky new false teeth, and talking about this and that and daily matters. I wrote my poems, showing them to no-one. A member of my family had found and read a story I wrote and voiced the strong opinion that I would never be a writer. Sometimes when I began to say what I *really* felt, using a simile or metaphor, an image, I saw the embarrassment in my listener's eyes – here was the mad person speaking.

During the early weeks of my stay in Sunnyside I had corresponded with John Forrest but his carboned letters, intended for family and friends, with their hearty *Dear Everyone* chilled me, and when during my stay in Oamaru I learned that he had married, I, with a natural sense of being excluded, no longer wrote the freely confessional letters in my style of being 'kin' to Van Gogh and Hugo Wolf, where I voiced my fantasies and described my behaviour.

My stay with my sister and her husband was not successful. They and their infant son enclosed one another while I stood awkwardly in the background and if anyone called and looked my way, my shyness and self-consciousness arising from my feeling of being nowhere, increased when my sister's friends asked, 'How is she?' 'Does she like being in Auckland?' I had become a third person, at home at Willowglen and now here in Auckland. Sometimes, as if I were my own obituary, people asked, 'What was she?' As if an archeological find stood before them and they were applying with eyes, heart and mind, a 'carbon' test to name, date and *place* me – and if only I had a place! It seemed to be and it was years since the Caxton Press had accepted my stories for publication. I had forgotten about them.

I could no longer bear the nothingness. I retreated to an inward state, that is, I put on such a mask, while at the same time totally aware of everything. I, in my nothingness and nowhereness was asserting the nothingness and nowhereness of everything and everyone around me. Such a condition, of course, led to my removal to the Auckland Mental Hospital at Avondale; at least it was a 'place' for me where I was believed to be 'at home'. I quickly fitted into my adopted country, again speaking the language fluently. The squalor and inhumanity were almost indescribable. I retain many many scenes of the crowded dayroom and exercise yard, and were I to rewrite *Faces in the Water* I would include much that I omitted because I did not want a record by a former patient to appear to be over-dramatic. The admission ward, Ward Seven (?) is remembered as an oasis with its park and willowtree and its friendly ward sister and no-one would ever have dreamed that beyond it stood the buildings known as *Park House*, where human beings became or were quickly transformed into living as animals.

The years spent there were compressed with tragedy and often with humour although the prevailing mood was one of a doomed eternity, all hope abandoned.

During my stay in Avondale my book of stories, *The Lagoon*, was published. I had been transferred to the admission ward. I was thin, with sores, and a discharging ear; everyone in Park House had sores or infected limbs and, in spite of the weekly combing with kerosene, some had lice. I was in bed in the admission ward when my sister and her husband brought me my six free copies of *The Lagoon*. I spread them on the white government counterpane embroidered with the New Zealand coat of arms: Ake Ake, Onward, Onward. I thought the appearance of the book was beautiful with its pale blue design like links of stalks of wild grass. I turned the pages, feeling the tiny grains within the paper.

'What shall I do with them?' I asked.

Knowing more about such things than I, they explained that if you were an author you signed your name beneath the printing of your name.

'Really?' I was impressed.

I signed my name in each copy, giving them away to those who, they suggested, 'ought to have a copy', keeping one for myself. My book. *The Lagoon and Other Stories*. The Caxton Press, not I, had decided the title.

It was then arranged that as my sister and her husband were about to visit the South Island, I should go with them home to Oamaru. My sister would fly with me and her two young sons, while her husband would drive from Auckland, arriving in Oamaru about ten days later.

During the flight to Oamaru there was a change of plane at Christchurch and while we waited, I, with my book still large in my mind, scanned a copy of the Christchurch *Press*, the book page, to see what 'they' were saying about my new book. Towards the foot of the page, compressed into five or six lines, the review dismissed *The Lagoon and Other Stories* with phrases like 'This kind of thing has been done before, too often . . . no originality . . . a waste of time to publish such a book.' The literary critics of the time, having been persuaded that our literature had 'come of age', found themselves embarrassed by so many writers writing of childhood: they supposed, How could a nation be adult if it wrote of its childhood? The longing for 'maturity' was desperate, partly because, among other terms for stages of growth, maturity was a fashionable word.

Reading the *Press* review, I felt painful humiliation and rejection, an increased torment of not knowing where to *be* – if I could not live within the world of writing books, then where could I survive?

My sister's visit to Willowglen, with her two small sons, was an illuminating disaster. With apparently nostalgic greed for power over the young, my father pounced upon the boys, watching their every move, indeed, refusing to allow them to make a move without his uttering a sharp, 'Now, now,' and reverting to long disused phrases like, 'You'll feel the back of my hand in a moment,' 'You do that once more and I'll skin you alive.' The boys were about three and one-and-a-half years and they were passionate rivals for possession of everything, from toys to attention. They became the focus of powerful feeling in all the adults. They were watched as if they were on exhibit; talked about, criticized, warned, reprimanded, described, and their future planned. My father watched them as he used to watch our cats when rarely he would allow them inside to play in the kitchen while we grouped about them to share the enjoyment of their play, until suddenly, Dad, the commander, would shout, like a king overseeing his jesters – Enough! Out!

And the cats would be thrust, meowing and bewildered, into the cold night while our enjoyment turned to disappointment and sadness.

I, as the acknowledged misfit in the family, felt the humiliation of seeing my mother talking intimately with my sister about marriage and bed and birth, where she had never dared to discuss these with me, and in later years when from time to time my sister would say, talking of a part of mother which I never knew, 'When Myrtle was being born . . . before Bruddie came . . .' I would feel like a child excluded from her mother's attention. Always in our family there was the struggle between powerlessness and power where closeness to people and the ability to prove that closeness became a symbol of most power, as if each member of the family struggled constantly to move through a wilderness of deprivation, slowly planting tiny cherished blossoms in the waste, and needing to point to them, describe them, rejoice in them, to the other members of the family who might not be so advanced in their journey through the desert. And an insight comes at last where each understands why the others must at times behave or speak with apparent glee at misfortune, or carefully set out the distances accomplished, naming the winners and the losers.

No letters came for me that summer. Who would be writing letters to me? My sister and her husband and the two wailing children flew north to their home. I was once again the mad Frame girl wandering the hills around the Old Mill with my cat Siggy who enjoyed long walks.

I slept in the front room overlooking the flat.

'I don't want you ever to leave home again,' Dad said. He built shelves for my books: my *Speaking For Ourselves*, *A Book of New Zealand Verse*, *Poetry London*, *Poetry in Wartime*, *Deaths and Entrances*, *The Waste Land*, Rilke's *Sonnets to Orpheus* (bought in Christchurch), Shakespeare (given to me in Christchurch by June and Wilson); and others, including my copy of *The Lagoon*. Dad gave me money to buy cretonne from Hodges, to make bright curtains for my room, while Mother bought from Calder Mackays ('we are valued customers') a new rose-coloured eiderdown for my bed.

All setting the family scene.

If I talked of my time in hospital, I described only the amusing incidents and the stereotypes of patients – the Jesus Christ, the Queen, the Empress.

Dad built up his supply of Sexton Blake library books. ('Janet likes detective stories.')

Mother and I composed recipes to send to *Truth* where we won first prize with a *Salmon Mousse*.

And although Dad treasured his flowers – the asters and dahlias and carnations staked in the small garden outside my window, he restrained his anger each time Siggy scratched among the dahlias or leapt from my bedroom window upon the frail stalks of the carnations. She would climb in the window at night and snuggle purring, at the foot of my bed, while I leaned down to stroke her black fur; whispering. Oh Siggy, Siggy, what will I do?

15
Threading Needles

The answer was decided for me. I found work as a laundry assistant at the Oamaru Public Hospital where I spent each day enclosed in the mangle room drawing out the hot wet sheets as they appeared between the rollers, folding them, and passing them to another assistant. Our faces in the steamy heat were flushed and sweating, and the conversation above the roar of the machinery was usually a shouted question and answer ('Are you going to the Scottish this Saturday?' 'Are you coming to Mary's shower?') enlarged upon during the tea breaks when the desirability of the 'Scottish' (a hall used for weekly dances) was debated, and Mary's or Vivian's or Noeline's engagement 'shower' prepared for. I had no answers to the simplest questions: where had I been working before I came to the laundry? Was I 'going out' with anyone? Why didn't I get my hair straightened? I could discuss the radio serial, *My Husband's Love*, which we listened to at ten o'clock each morning. I knew one or two racehorses, including *Plunder Bar*. I knew songs – 'Give Me Five Minutes More',

> Only five minutes more,
> Let me stay
> Let me stay in your arms,
> All the week I've dreamed about our Saturday date . . .

an outworn song even then, but I knew it. And I knew the names of Otago and Southland Rugby favourites – the Trevathans, and the commentator, *Whang McKenzie*. I felt out of place, however. (Siggy, Siggy, what will I do?)

Then one night, in the middle of the night, mother had a heart attack. Waking, hearing the commotion, I was reminded of the night when Bruddie first became ill and we all woke and stood white-faced, shivering.

Now Bruddie came to my door where I stood in alarm. He spoke in the new tone used now by Dad and Bruddie when they spoke to me, as if I had to be 'managed' in some way, for fear I should break or respond in an unusual way which they could not deal with.

'It's alright. There's nothing to worry about. Mum has had a heart attack. The doctor has given her morphine and they're taking her to the hospital.'

I looked out to see mother, seeming asleep, her face white as china, her long grey-white hair spread anyhow on the white pillow, being carried out on a stretcher. She opened her eyes and started to apologize for having fallen ill; then she closed them again. Dad and Bruddie went with her to the hospital, and I went back to bed. There was a dent at the foot of the bed where Siggy had been, and had leapt with fright out of the window. I looked out of the window into the tree-filled dark. I heard the three o'clock morepork calling. And already the night was fading around the edges. I knew it was a night of the kind of violent change that always happens, and had appeared as a milestone in the landscape of our family.

In the morning, as it had been years ago on the first morning after Bruddie's illness began, I woke remembering the complex fearful change in our lives. I longed for everything to be as it had been, with mother quiet, self-effacing, providing; but it was not so; mother had spoken at last, in pain. What if she died? No, they had said, with plenty of rest she would recover, although *in future* she would need to rest more, care more for herself, be cared for.

And while she rested warm and safe in the hospital, I could see the desolation in my father's face – Dad, who always showed panic whenever he entered the kitchen and said, 'Where's Mum?' and she was not there, even for the moment not there, perhaps in another room or out at the clothesline; but now she was gone from the house, and my father's face showed his complete loss and bewilderment.

I made the breakfast. I brewed the everlasting pots of tea for Dad crouched in his chair at his end of the table, but I did not extend my attention to the refinements he sought, demanded, from mother – the tea sugared, stirred, shoes cleaned, back scratched. I heated the electric iron to iron his handkerchiefs and his shirt. He set his own blueys to soak in the wash-house tub, poking them with the copper-stick. He also set and lit the fire and fetched the shovels of railway coal from the heap in the lean-to by the back door.

Mother had spoken at last; in pain. The magic of fires in the coal range, hot meals, batches of pikelets cooked on the polished black girdle, the continued attendance of the servant upon the household, was over.

How dare she fall ill! We were desperate to have her returned to us, returned whole without pain.

I saw mother in hospital. For the first time, as a result of her complete, dramatic removal from her family, I saw her as a person, and I was afraid and resentful. Why, she was a person such as you meet in the street. She could laugh and talk and express opinions without being ridiculed; and there she was, writing poems in a small notebook and reading them to the other patients who were impressed with her talent.

'Your mother writes lovely poems.'

What had we done to her, each of us, day after day, year after year, that we had washed away her evidence of self, all her own furniture from her own room, and crowded it with our selves and our lives; or perhaps it was not a room but a garden that we cleared to plant ourselves deeply there, and now that we were removed, all her own blossoms had sprung up . . . was it like that? And what of the blows she had, the search for cures, the two inquests, the daughter declared mad, the frail husband made strong only by his intermittent potions of cruelty?

Faced with the family anguish I made my usual escape, the route now perfected, and once again I was in Seacliff Hospital. I knew as soon as I arrived there that the days of practising that form of escape were over. I would go away somewhere, live on my own, earn enough money to live on, write my books: it was no use: I now had what was known as a 'history', and ways of dealing with those with a 'history' were stereotyped, without investigation. Very quickly, in my panic, I was removed to the back ward, the Brick Building where I became one of the forgotten people. When mother recovered her health, she and Bruddie and Dad would visit me for Christmas and my birthday and on one or two other occasions during the year. It was recognized that I was now in hospital 'for life'. What I have described in Istina Mavet is my sense of hopelessness as the months passed, my fear of having to endure that constant state of physical capture where I was indeed at the mercy of those who made judgements and decisions without even talking at length to me or trying to know me or even submitting me to the standard tests which are available to psychiatrists. The state could be defined as forced submission to custodial capture.

In the back ward I became part of a memorable family that I have described individually in *Faces in the Water*. It was their sadness and courage and my desire to 'speak' for them that enabled me to survive, helped by the insight of such fine junior and staff nurses as Cassidy, Doherty (both Maori women), 'Taffy', the Welsh nurse now living in Cardiff, Noreen Ramsay (who gave me extra food when I was hungry), and others. The attitude of those in charge who unfortunately wrote the reports and influenced the treatment was that of reprimand and punishment, with certain forms of medical treatment being threatened as punishment for failure to 'co-operate' where 'not co-operate' might mean a refusal to obey an order, say, to go to the doorless lavatories with six others and urinate in public while suffering verbal abuse by the nurse for being unwilling. 'Too fussy are we? Well, Miss Educated, you'll learn a thing or two here.'

Dear Educated, Miss Educated: sadly, the fact of my having been to High School, Training College, and University struck a vein of vindictiveness among some of the staff.

It was my writing that at last came to my rescue. It is little wonder that I value writing as a way of life when it actually saved my life. My mother had been persuaded the sign permission for me to undergo a leucotomy; I know that she would not have done so had not the experts wielded heavily weighted arguments – the experts, who over the years as my 'history' was accumulating, had not spoken to me at one time for longer than ten or fifteen minutes, and in total time over eight years, for about eighty minutes; who had administered no tests, not even the physical tests of EEG or X-rays (apart from the chest X-ray whenever there was a new case of tuberculosis, a disease prevalent in the mental hospitals then); the experts whose judgement was based on daily reports by overworked irritable nursing sisters. I listened, trying to avoid the swamping wave of horror, when Dr Burt, a likeable overworked young doctor who had scarcely spoken to me except to say 'good morning, how are you' and not wait for a reply as he was whisked through the ward, *found time* to explain that I would be having a leucotomy operation, that it would be good for me, that, following it, I would be 'out of hospital in no time.' I listened also with a feeling that my erasure was being completed when the ward sister, suddenly interested that something was about to be 'done' with and to me, painted her picture of how I would be when it was 'all over'.

'We had one patient who was here for years until she had a leucotomy. And now she's selling hats in a hat shop. I saw her just the other day, selling hats, as normal as anyone. Wouldn't you like to be normal?'

Everyone felt that it was better for me to be 'normal' and not have fancy intellectual notions about being a writer, that it was better for me to be out of hospital, working at an ordinary occupation, mixing with others . . .

The scene was carefully set. A young woman of my age who had become a friend but who had remained in the admission ward, the 'good' ward, was also spoken of as about to have a leucotomy.

'Nola's having one,' they told me.

Nola's having her hair straightened, Nola's having a party dress, Nola's having a party – why not you too?

Nola suffered from asthma and the complication of being in a family of brilliant beautiful people. I can make no judgement on her 'case' except to say that in a period before the use of drugs, leucotomy was becoming a 'convenience' treatment.

I repeat that my writing saved me. I had seen in the ward office the list of those 'down for a leucotomy', with my name on the list, and other names being crossed off as the operation was performed.

My 'turn' must have been very close when one evening the superintendent of the hospital, Dr Blake Palmer, made an unusual visit to the ward. He spoke to me – to the amazement of everyone.

As it was my first chance to discuss with anyone, apart from those who had persuaded me, the prospect of my operation, I said urgently, 'Dr Blake Palmer, what do you think?'

He pointed to the newspaper in his hand.

'About the prize?'

I was bewildered. What prize? 'No,' I said, 'about the leucotomy.'

He looked stern. 'I've decided that you should stay as you are. I don't want you changed.' He unfolded his newspaper. 'Have you seen the Stop Press in tonight's *Star*?'

A ridiculous question to ask in a back ward where there was no reading matter; surely he knew?

'You've won the Hubert Church Award for the best prose. Your book, *The Lagoon*.'

I knew nothing about the Hubert Church Award. Winning it was obviously something to be pleased about.

I smiled. 'Have I?'

'Yes. And we're moving you out of this ward. And no leucotomy.'

The winning of the prize and the attention of a new doctor from Scotland who accepted me as I appeared to him and not as he learned about me from my 'history' or reports of me, and the move by Dr Blake Palmer to have me spend less time in the hospital ward by using me as 'tea lady' in the front office, and allowing me to have occupational therapy where I learned to make baskets, to fill toothpaste tubes with toothpaste, and, from a book written in French, to weave French lace, and to weave on large and small looms, all enabled me to be prepared for discharge from hospital. Instead of being treated by leucotomy, I was treated as a person of some worth, a human being, in spite of the misgivings and unwillingness of some members of the staff who, like certain relatives when a child is given attention, warn the mother that the child is being 'spoiled', spoke pessimistically and perhaps enviously of my being 'made a fuss of'. 'It will spoil her. Dr Blake Palmer will "drop" her and she'll be back in the Brick Building in no time.'

My friend Nola who unfortunately had not won a prize, whose name did not appear in the newspaper, had her leucotomy, and was returned to the hospital where, among the group known as 'the leucotomies', some attempt was made to continue, with personal attention, the process of 'being made normal, or at least being changed.' The 'leucotomies' were talked to, taken for walks, prettied with make-up and floral scarves covering their shaven heads. They were silent, docile; their eyes were large and dark and their faces pale, with damp skin. They were being 'retrained', to 'fit in' to the everyday world, always described as 'outside'; 'the world outside.' In the whirlwind of work and the shortage of staff and the too-slow process of retraining, the leucotomies one by one became the casualties of withdrawn attention and interest; the false spring turned once again to winter.

When I was eventually discharged from hospital, Nola remained, and although she did spend time out of hospital, she was often re-admitted; over the years I kept in touch with her, and it was like living in a fairytale where conscience, and what might-have-been, and what was, not only speak but spring to life and become a living companion, a reminder.

Nola died a few years ago in her sleep. The legacy of her dehumanizing change remains no doubt with all those who knew her; I have it with me always.

I was discharged from hospital 'on probation'. After having received over two hundred applications of unmodified ECT, each the equivalent, in degree of fear, to an execution, and in the process having my memory shredded and in some aspects weakened permanently or destroyed, and after having been subjected to proposals to have myself changed, by a physical operation, into a more acceptable, amenable, normal person, I arrived home at Willowglen, outwardly smiling and calm, but inwardly with all confidence gone, with the conviction at last that I was officially a non-person. I had seen enough of schizophrenia to know that I had never suffered from it, and I had long discarded the prospect of inevitable mental doom. Against this opinion, however, I now had the weight of the 'experts' and the 'world' and I was in no state to assert myself. There was the added fear of what might happen to me should I ever return to hospital. And there was still the fact, the problem that, had it been solved eight or nine years ago, I might have been left free to pursue the kind of life I felt I wanted to lead. A problem with such a simple solution! A place to live and write, with enough money to support myself.

There was also the frightening knowledge that the desire to write, the enjoyment of writing, has little correlation with talent. Might I not, after all, be deluding myself like other patients I had seen in hospital, one in particular, a harmless young woman who quietly sat in the admission ward day after day writing her 'book' because she wanted to be a writer, and her book, on examination, revealing pages and pages of pencilled 0-0-0-0-0-0-0-0. Or was that the new form of communication?

In spite of all, I felt joyful returning to Willowglen where I could at last go out under the sky, where I could perform even the simplest of human functions without either being ordered to do so or observed while I performed. I could *decide* for myself what I wished to do, where I should be, how I should feel, how I should think of my *future*. The words *decide* and *future* which had loomed so large in my childhood had a new intensity of meaning.

After being and feeling a nothing and nobody, and forced into a continued state of physical and emotional submission, I felt as if the world would sweep over and engulf me, while I would meekly accept and act upon suggestions and orders from others, out of the habitual fear that had grown within me, in hospital.

Ah, but it was a delight to roam the hills again with my now many-kittened Siggie, to sit near the matagouri among the sheep, and try to forget everything but the sky swept with its arrows of cirrus clouds that I used to try so hard to draw with my double B pencil. I borrowed a small tent from Bruddie who had been having his own adventures in New Zealand and Australia while I was in hospital. I pitched the tent under the pine trees, so great was my need to be among the trees and under the sky, and at night I slept in the tent and during the day I sat writing in the railway notebook given to me by my father in his sad haste to make all as it used to be, everyone small again and he the king of the world. He had retired from the railway and was now working as an engine driver at the lime works, coming home each day clouded with white dust as if he had been in a snow storm.

My time sleeping in a tent was cut short. Wasn't it rather . . . strange . . . for me to want to sleep in a tent . . . people were talking . . . I gave up the tent for my old bedroom up at the house.

'It's nice to have Janet home again,' people said, in my presence. 'How is she? Would she like some shortbread?'

I joined the new town library and discovered William Faulkner and Franz Kafka, and I rediscovered the few books left on my own bookshelf. I began to write stories and poems and to think of a future without being overcome by fear that I would be seized and 'treated' without being able to escape. Even so, the nightmares of my time in hospital persist in sleep and often I wake in dread, having dreamed that the nurses are coming to 'take me for treatment'.

Mother's health had improved under the care of Professor Smirk of Dunedin. Periodically she visited his clinic and was admitted for short stays in hospital where once again she became a 'person' in the company of those who were not members of the family. Although scarcely sixty years old and still dreaming of buying her daughters a white fox fur, she was worn out by her living (I thought) for her husband and children, as if without her own life, like a stake cut from a grand tree, stripped of its own shoots and set beside flourishing plants, bound to them, taking the force of the prevailing wind, moving only as the wind moved while the sheltered plants trembled lightly with only a rumour of storm. My vision of my mother combined strangely with her presence – her white thinning hair, her toothless mouth, for she had never been fitted with comfortable false teeth, her hawklike Godfrey nose pointed towards her Godfrey chin, or, as we used to say, her 'Archbishop of Canterbury' chin, her used body in its Glassons Warehouse costume (it was her delight that Mabel Howard also bought clothes from Glassons) and McDiarmids 'on tick' wide-bodied shoes, her face serene as ever and her eyes always waiting to sparkle with humour about political or personal events. She had given up the Christadelphian meetings, disillusioned by too much quarrelling among the Pacifists but she was still a Christadelphian, *lover of Christ.* During the years of her married life Christ had been her one close friend. She still talked, however, and listed her childhood friends, 'Hetty Peake, Ruby Blake, Kate Rodley, Lucy Martella, Dorcas Dryden.' She remembered her boyfriends, too. And when Dad's friend from the Wyndham days, Johnny and his wife retired to live near us in Oamaru, mother's diffidence made her unable to address Mrs Walker as *Bessie.* The strong feeling haunted me that mother had never lived in her real 'place', that her real world had been her life within.

Her eyesight was now failing. Sewing buttons on the shirts and pyjamas, and stitching the frayed cuffs of the 'menfolk', she had to ask for help in threading her needle. I sat sewing, too, and my thread through my needle was keen and swift as a tiny spear. 'Janet, can you thread the needle for me?' and with an inside fury at this sign of her helplessness, I took the needle, not gently, and threaded it with the lightning accuracy of my twenty-ninth year. She had never aspired, against the glories of her sisters-in-law, to be a needlewoman, nor had she time during the years to sit and sew, while we girls had long ago been makers for better or worse of our own clothes; and to see mother helpless in a role which had scarcely claimed her once-keen eyesight, reserved for matters of the heart and spirit, for poetry, for the making of fires and the preparation of food, for looking at her beloved 'nature', I felt the terrible reduction in her life, a final subtraction which I could not bear to face. I knew, also, that I would never be close to her, for my past and my future life were barriers against the intimacy that grows between mother and daughter.

I could postpone my future no longer. I answered an advertisement for a housemaid at the Grand Hotel, Dunedin, my references being an old letter from the Mayor of Oamaru, and the reference from Playfair Street, Caversham, 'polite to the guests at all times ... honest ... industrious ...' and once again, moving towards my Future, I travelled south on the slow train to Dunedin.

PART TWO
Finding the Silk

Separated from time as a silkworm from the silk.

16
Grand Hotel

I was about to live in Dunedin for the third time since I had left
school, and each time, first with the months and now with the
intervening years and experience a difference had been wrought in
my relation with the city that was now one of my oldest acquaintances, perhaps my only acquaintance. A curious process of scouring
had occurred – the removal of the surface wonder of being a
student; then, from the second visit, the days of anguish, of
discovering schizophrenia, and music, and handsome young men,
and writing my stories and trying to appear mad in poetic fashion,
still clinging to the wreckage of my teaching career, wandering by
the Leith, imposing upon myself an exaggerated sense of the
tragedy of *me* – these too had gone, taking the spirit of Jude and
Christminster, of the Scholar Gypsy and Oxford,

> Have I not pass'd thee on the wooden bridge,
> Wrapt in thy cloak and battling with the snow,
> Thy face towards Hinksey and its wintry ridge?
> And thou hast climb'd the hill,
> And gain'd the white brow of the Cumner range;
> Turn'd once to watch while thick the snowflakes fall,
> The line of festal light in Christ-Church hall –

of all who ever dreamed by university rivers and old buildings of
grey stone.

Now, on my third visit to live in Dunedin, the University and
Training College were no longer my world: I had no world.
Union Street, Frederick Street, Dundas Street, all the former
surroundings were like toy streets with toy buildings where the toy
people had been replaced by new toy people, still talking and
laughing about the old topics.

I took a taxi from the railway station to the Grand Hotel standing tall on the corner, with its varnished wood and polished brass, like a handsome ship. The manageress, dignified but slightly drunk, met me in the foyer, explaining that there'd been a mistake, it was a *waitress* they needed, not a housemaid.

'You may wish to go elsewhere, then, Miss Frame,' she said while I, already uncurling my dormant bruised roots, said quickly, trying not to feel too frightened and dismayed, 'Oh, I have experience of waitressing. I'll be a waitress.'

'The pay is six pounds a week clear, all found.'

All found.

Like a child's refrain: All gone, All found.

My room was an attic room on the top floor looking out through the small window beyond the battlement kind of façade, to Princes Street and across to dental rooms and insurance offices. All the staff had rooms on the top floor.

I wore a starched white smock, white shoes and a starched cap. I was given a 'station' or set of tables to wait upon and I quickly learned the language and the behaviour that was expected of me. I learned the routine as well, from the attitude to adopt towards the head waitress, the manager and his wife (who startled me by their resemblance to those I had known in Christchurch until I realized that such jobs were taken by persons of similar appearance and nature), to the kitchen routine and the setting of tables, the special way to fold the serviettes into their rosette. I learned also to sense the excitement among my fellow waitresses when guests were leaving and there was the hope that a tip would be left under the plate. The regular guests, the good tippers, were known, and there was rivalry to have them seated at one's station but Doreen, the head waitress, a small fair woman in black with lace collar and cuffs, arranged the seating for important guests and then often took over the station, collecting the final trophies of service. There were sharp glances between waitresses, moments of anxiety as the guests set aside their plates, and a planned carelessness about the approach to the table and the discreet lifting of the plate and pocketing of the tip. I felt ashamed of my rising excitement on the day a guest was to leave, and of my concealed eager greed as I eased the tip into my hand, holding it there until I could sneak it, unobserved, into my pocket.

The Grand Hotel was a congenial place to work. I enjoyed walking about the dining room in my uniform with the table napkin draped over my arm. I took pride in remembering the orders, and stacking the plates to be carried. The staff had freedom to make their own arrangements about holidays and working hours and often I'd be able to exchange with another waitress, to have two or three days free, when I'd go home to Willowglen, or stay at the hotel, relishing the security of a place to sleep, good meals, and earnings of six pounds a week *clear*. I bought a secondhand typewriter and began to write stories and poems. I wrote 'The Waitresses', 'The Liftman', poems that were published in the *Listener*. I wrote about Kafka and about a concert by the Alma Trio, and a poem 'On Paying the First Instalment', a result of a rash move into the world of time payment, when I bought a radiogram and one record, Beethoven's Seventh Symphony which I'd heard on the radio concert programme, and which I now could play softly in my attic refuge. The Dance. For me, it *was* the dance, filled with a special joy and freedom with the strong beat in the last movement seeming like the wielding of a crystal hammer fit for the construction of a palace of crystal, without walls, the air and light flowing through it from all corners of earth and heaven.

Away from my refuge I gradually lost my honeymoon delight in the world of waitressing. To protect myself from questions about my 'past', I made it known that I was 'really a student' and 'hoping to be a writer'. I was unhappily aware that, not feeling myself to have a 'place' in the world, and being unwilling to accept that I existed in any place, I was inclined to adopt, when questioned, the air of a secret princess among the scullions; but not in public; only if one of the staff came to my room to talk over boyfriend problems, and should she, if he was married, and what else was there to do, a life of waitressing and ending up like T or M.

Then I'd be asked, 'And what about you? What are you doing here?'

And I'd say that I'd written a book but as I had no copy of *The Lagoon*, many of my books having vanished when I was looked on as being in hospital for life, that is, dead, my fellow waitresses were sceptical. I showed them my poem, 'The Waitresses', printed in the *Listener*, under my initials.

Their chief desire, however, was to make me one of them, to join with them in their activities.

'Your hair, your clothes, they're awful. And your lipstick's the wrong colour. You have to be careful what colour you wear, with your red hair. Never red – it clashes. Greens and browns. Or blue to go with your blue eyes. Why don't you come with us to the Saturday night dance at the Town Hall? And why don't you get your hair straightened? It would be much better, straightened.'

After years of being in the command of others, with threat of punishment by solitary confinement or 'treatment' if I disobeyed or, to use the official term, 'became unco-operative', I was willing to accept any suggestions. Green and brown became *my* colours. I daringly went to the cosmetic counter at the DIC where the assistant, testing lipsticks on the back of my hand, chose 'my' shade of 'Tangee'. I bought rose milk for my skin, and Evening in Paris perfume in its deep blue bottle. And seeing my efforts to 'make something of myself', as they expressed it, the other waitresses were pleased. 'Now you're one of us,' they said.

After work we sat talking about our clothes, our hair, our boss and his wife, and each other, and how Mabel was dotty, and Laura was a bit 'funny' – who'd believe that tale of her engagement to the taxi driver when he never came near her? Who indeed? I thought, for Mabel and Laura were only two of the mental misfits who drift without much sympathy or help, from hotel to hostel and boardinghouse, finding a temporary home, and work, for 'so much a week and all found.' I felt myself to be one of them: where else could they live?

My honeymoon delight finally ended in the hotel kitchen. The servings of dinner were different for men and women, with men given a larger portion, and, of chicken, the *leg* or *wing*, while women were served a smaller portion, and always *breast* of chicken, and thus when I came through the swing doors to call out my order I had to shout swiftly, *Chicken, a gent* or *chicken, a lady. Beef, a gent, Beef, a lady*. My voice was soft, I was reluctant to shout, and I

118

found the word *gent* distasteful. I therefore made my order, *Chicken, a man, beef, a man*, overturning all the tradition of the kitchen of the Grand Hotel. Chicken, a man, indeed!

The second cook, a brusque bully, launched a teasing, angry attack on my language and refused to fill my orders unless I gave them in the traditional way, and sensing my reluctance, she insisted that I repeat my order again and again. The giving of meal orders became a torment. One day I ran in tears from the servery, up to my attic room, and when Pat, the waitress, came to my room, I said I wasn't well.

I wondered what I could do, where I could go. There was nowhere. I tried to be calm. I was free, wasn't I, no longer locked up. Was I free?

That evening I returned to the dining room.

'Don't take any notice of Molly, she's like that,' Pat whispered as we stood by the sideboard waiting for the guests to come in. 'They're late this evening. We'll be ages getting away. But don't take any notice of Molly.'

Pat was tall with dark curly hair. Her ambition was to go up north to manage a cake shop, and perhaps buy it.

'Are you coming to the Town Hall dance tomorrow night?' she asked. 'We're all going.'

I had bought some of the latest material, *everglaze* which was all the rage, and a pattern from the DIC, and I was sewing by hand a dress to wear some night to the dance. That evening Pat inspected my dress, and helped me with the hem of the circular skirt.

'Circular skirts are hard to turn up.'

'Are you really going to be a writer?' Pat asked.

'I hope so.'

'Don't take any notice of Molly in the kitchen. Second cooks are always like that. The first cook lords it over everyone, the second cook throws her weight around and the third cook does all the work. I felt awful when I first come here to work. I'd had a nervous breakdown, you see.'

'I've been in a mental hospital,' I said, bursting into tears.

The next evening Pat and I and two of the others all dressed up to kill, I in my new everglaze dress with the circular skirt and the leg-of-mutton sleeves, set out for the Town Hall two blocks away.

'Isn't it great, living in a hotel, you can just walk anywhere?'

The Town Hall dance had begun, the band was playing, there was the shuffling sound of the dancers on the powdered floor, but so far the dancers were few. A line of men stood against one wall; a line of women against the opposite wall self-consciously waited for the men to ask them to dance while the men looked them over, making jumping and jerking movements, half-pawing the floor with their feet, like prize bulls at the Show.

I sat with the other girls from the hotel. One by one they were invited to dance. I remained seated, still full of pleasurable anticipation, nodding my head to the music, tapping my feet as a way of showing anyone who might be looking my way that I was eager to dance; but not too eager, not so as to forget I had pride, though how much pride can you have when you must wait to be asked?

I had a secret: this was my first dance, apart from the hospital dances where I had learned many steps and where I'd had two faithful partners – the bald middle aged man old enough to be my father, and the sad young ex-soldier, dark and handsome, who still believed he was in Italy fighting the Second World War. When I was a child, I was always excited by the adventures of a *first time*, and eager to share it with others. Now, I had missed so many experiences in ordinary living that my 'firsts', out of step with the 'firsts' of others, were felt to be a cause for shame. Also, I had read eagerly in the literature of first dances, including the story by Katherine Mansfield; but even her title, 'Her First Ball', had been given a crude interpretation by my sisters and me, as the young farmers who partnered Isabel to the woolshed 'hops' out in the country were apt to make remarks, picked up quickly by Isabel, about Farmers' Balls, Shearers' Balls, and so on, and the word 'ball' no longer applied to mother's dreamed-of Viennese Night.

It *was* an occasion – my first dance; the sweaty smell, the chatter, the music; the shiny noses being blotted with a powder puff. I had sewn rubber shields in the armpits of my dress, and I could feel the sticky rubber against my arms. I still sat, patiently waiting, watching the dancers and trying to appear as if this were the reason for my being in the Town Hall – to watch the dancers. Ah, there was the Maxina, the Military Twostep, and – oh – the Destiny. I knew those. Ask me, ask me. An older woman sat beside me and began to talk.

'We could go upstairs and watch them. You get a good view from upstairs.'

I moved away to another seat. How dare she, how dare she assume that I was just like her, frumpy and not dancing! Even dotty Laura was dancing. And there was a row of men who still hadn't asked anyone. My pleasurable feeling began to fade exposing its original surface of pain, a dull disappointment and hurt. I fiddled with my new evening bag that was black with sparkles – sequins – oh for a dress, oh for a bag with sequins! I snipped open the bag and looked at my Max Factor compact and my Evening in Paris perfume. Then I shut the bag and trying to look calm, I walked from the Town Hall into the Octagon and down into Princes Street and home to the *Grand*. So much for my attempt and failure at living in the world, I thought, as I played my record of the Seventh Symphony. The dance. I heard the others coming in late, making a cup of coffee or tea, laughing, talking. They'd had fun. And when, the next morning, they asked me, 'How'd you like the dance?' I answered, 'It was great, wasn't it?'

They agreed. 'It was a great dance.'

17

Mr Brasch and Landfall

Sometimes I browsed in Modern Books (the old Co-operative Book Society) where I hoped to glimpse one of the literary figures of Dunedin or one visiting from up north. I now knew by heart most of the stories from *Speaking For Ourselves*, as well as the biographical notes on the writers and the introductory chapter which, like the introduction to the *Book of New Zealand Verse*, became my primer of New Zealand literature. I accepted every judgement without question: if a poem or story was said to be the 'best', then I believed it to be so, and searching it for proof, I always found proof. These two books were among my few links with 1945.

I bought a copy of *Landfall* and read it with awe – there was *avante garde* Maurice Duggan writing sentences without verbs, even one-noun sentences; and using italics; and painting New Zealand scenes unfamiliar to me, mostly from up north, with the subtropical heat crackling on the pages, and the old jetties rotting and the mangroves deep in grey mud; he seemed to relish writing about the mangroves; and about long-haired women in bedrooms; and everything that glistened – leaves and skin and water: that was up north.

The poems of *Landfall* were obscure, scholarly, very carefully written with formal stanzas and intricate rhyme and rhythm; occasionally there was a rogue free verse of half-a-dozen lines. I sensed that if you didn't appear in *Landfall* then you could scarcely call yourself a writer.

Then one day I saw Charles Brasch standing behind the counter selling books. Charles Brasch, the poet! I thought,

Speak for us, great sea.
Speak in the night, compelling
The frozen heart to hear,
The memoried to forget.
O speak, until your voice
Possess the night, and bless
The separate and fearful.

I bought a book of Allen Curnow's poems. I noted that Mr Brasch looked approvingly as he wrapped it for me. Then he said, as if startled, 'Oh. You're Janet Frame? Do you live in Dunedin now?'

'I've been here a few months. I live and work at the Grand Hotel.'

He looked uneasy, and said again, 'Oh.'

He then asked if I would like to come to his place for tea one afternoon. I looked shy.

'Yes.'

'What about this Thursday? At half-past three?'

'Yes, that will be alright.'

He gave me his address in Royal Terrace. He had a poet's eyes, a soft voice, and thick black hair. I remembered his poems in the *Book of New Zealand Verse*: they were mysterious poems, questions addressed to the mountains, the sea, and the dead, with the sad certainty that here would be no answer.

'I'll see you on Thursday, then. And remember, if you have anything to contribute to *Landfall*, you can always leave it at the bookshop.'

'Yes,' I said, smiling shyly.

That evening I told Pat and Doreen that I was going to afternoon tea on Thursday at the house of a poet.

'He's one of our best poets,' I said.

'What will you wear?' they asked.

I was saving to buy a green coat I'd seen in the window of Mademoiselle Modes but I hadn't yet saved its price of ten pounds.

'I haven't a coat,' I said.

'Wear your jersey and skirt. And something to take away that bare look from your neck. Beads? Pearls would be better. You need pearls.'

'Where do you think I would get pearls?'

'Is the poet rich?' they asked.

'I've heard he is.'

'Well, you have nothing to worry about. Wear a brassiere though.'

The next day I went to the Fashion Centre in Moray Place where a heavily built woman in black with a black strip of velvet around her throat and pearl earrings like Aunty Isy's, ushered me into the fitting-room.

'Will you have plunging neckline or petal cups?'

The attention of the others and their interest in the afternoon tea embarrassed me. Soon everyone knew I was going. Even the liftman mentioned it. He too was one of the sad misfits for whom a working- and living-place like a hotel became a shelter and who, in the hotel surroundings, appeared strong and confident, yet who glimpsed in the street displayed like a banner the frailty and difference.

Thursday arrived, promising rain.

'Perhaps he will give you a coat,' someone said, 'if he knows you don't have one.'

I walked up the hill towards Royal Terrace. I was far too early. I loitered, looking down over the harbour and peninsula, picking out the landmarks of University, the Museum, half-glimpsed through trees, the Normal School, and, scarcely visible at the foot of Union Street, the Training College. I looked towards the Oval with its puddles and seagulls, and I thought of Number Four Garden Terrace and Aunty Isy who no longer lived there. Separated at last from the chocolate trophies of her dancing, she had turned to the source of her skill, her former dancing master, and after a brief courtship they were married and I had seen her with him, both laughing and happy, 'passing through' on the Limited, on their way to live in Mangakino, in a house without trees in the garden.

I looked towards Caversham. I thought of the house in Playfair Street, blocked from view by the grim shape of Parkside Home for the Aged. And I thought of the Carisbrook football ground and Whang McKenzie announcing the teams at the 'Railway end' or the 'Cargill Road end' and *Whang*, it's a goal!

At last I found courage to knock on the door in Royal Terrace. Mr Brasch greeted me, then showed me to a large book-lined room where he served tea and seed cake while a white cat known as Whizz-Bang looked on. I told Mr Brasch that my mother had worked for old Mrs Beauchamp, Katherine Mansfield's grandmother, and for 'old Mr Fels', his own grandfather.

'She remembers you and your sister,' I said.

Mr Brasch looked stern. I felt that he disliked personal reminiscences and references, but what else could I say? I knew so little. He began to talk of New Zealand literature. I remained silent. I thought, He must know where I have been for the past eight years. I suddenly felt like crying. I was awkward and there were crumbs of seed cake all over my plate and on the white carpet at my feet. Then, remembering the introduction to *Speaking For Ourselves*, I murmured one or two opinions on the stories, quoting directly from the text.

'I agree with you,' Mr Brasch said.

Our conversation died away. Mr Brasch poured more tea from an attractive pot with a wicker handle arched above it.

'I'm fond of this teapot,' he said, noticing my glance at it.

'I'd better be going,' I said.

'Don't forget that if you have any stories or poems you can leave them at Modern Books.'

'Yes,' I said in a shy whisper.

When Mr Brasch opened the door, he said in a startled voice, 'Oh, it's raining, and you haven't a coat. Would you like a coat?'

'No thank you, I haven't far to go.'

When I returned to the Grand Hotel and my fellow workers asked about my visit, I said slyly, 'He offered me a coat.'

They were impressed.

'You should have worn pearls, though,' they said.

That week I typed a story and two poems for *Landfall*. The story, 'Gorse is Not People', dealt with a visit to Dunedin by another patient and myself in the company of a nurse. After many years in hospital, I had almost no clothes, possibly because my family's image of people in hospital was that of patients in bed wearing nightgowns; and in any case, my family could not afford to give me clothes; and I was reluctant to ask them; therefore the hospital authorities were sending me to Dunedin with a nurse who would buy me some underclothing and deal with the affairs of the other patient, a woman celebrating her twenty-first birthday, known as her 'majority'. She was Linda, a small wizened person who had been in hospital since her early childhood and whose explanation for her dwarf-like size was that she was 'illegitimate' and her mother had not wanted her to grow. Only the staff knew the reason for her being in hospital. The patients, myself among them, saw her as a small person, shrewd, tenacious of will, who was able to control many of the patients in the day room, either in the 'clean' day room or what was known as the 'dirty' day room. Linda also controlled the wireless with her choice of programme. For months she had been looking forward to her 'twenty-first' seeing in it the fulfilment of all her dreams, certain that when she became twenty-one she would be engaged, perhaps married, and allowed to 'get out of this dump'. In preparation for her engagement she had bought a pretty blue ring from the hospital store where we made our weekly visit to spend the five shillings personal allowance from the goverment. Linda was sure that her day in Dunedin was related to her coming engagement and freedom.

Her excitement was infectious. It was to be a wonderful day. Cakes, ice cream, perhaps the pictures with us sitting in a 'real audience'. And Linda, also with no-one to provide her with clothes, was to be fitted with a skirt and underwear.

My story tried to convey the reality of the visit. The nurse had explained to me that Linda was unaware of the reason for her being in Dunedin – she was to see a magistrate who would formally, now that she was twenty-one and adult, commit her to hospital 'for life'.

Even after our return from the city, Linda talked of the 'nice man' who had spoken to her 'specially' and who might have been her 'future husband, 'cept that he was too old. He knew I was grown up, though, that I'd had my twenty-first. I showed him my 'gagement ring, *saffirs*.'

The two poems I offered *Landfall* are best not remembered, their hand was so heavy. 'The Slaughter-House' began

> The mind entering the slaughter-house must remain
>   calm, never calmer,
> must be washed clean, showered on where the corned hide
> holds fast to bits of bacterial thought, must await the
>   stunning hammer
> in silence, knowing nothing of any future load.

Electric shock treatment may turn many grim memories out of house and home; what is certain is that it invites as permanent tenants the grim memories of itself, of receiving shock treatment.

I left the story and poems at the Modern Book shop, in an envelope addressed to Charles Brasch, and I returned to the Grand Hotel to await the response. I sat in my room inventing all possible judgements, imagining Charles Brasch in his book-lined room, opening the envelope, taking out the pages, unfolding them, reading them, and thinking, 'At last! Here's another writer of stories. We are indeed *Speaking for Ourselves*. What sensitivity! What subtle hints, never outright statements. The reference to the gorse is good – that chance remark of the nurse as the car leaves the *Kilmog* . . . What experiences this woman must have had (what tragic experiences!) to write in this way. A born writer.'

But – suppose he didn't think the work was good? Perhaps, like a school report, he would say, 'Can be improved. Not up to standard.'

I had made no copy of my story, to re-read it. What had I done?

Before the end of the week I received at the Grand Hotel a long bulky envelope containing my story and two poems. Mr Brasch's comments were that the work was interesting, but the poems were not quite suitable while the story, 'Gorse is Not People' was 'too painful to print'.

When I had read the note on its official *Landfall* paper, I began to realize how much I had invested in my *Landfall* contributions and their acceptance for publication. I seemed to have included my whole life and future in that envelope. I felt myself sinking into empty despair. What could I do if I couldn't write? Writing was to be my rescue. I felt as if my hands had been uncurled from their clinging-place on the rim of the lifeboat. My unhappiness was eased, however, by the knowledge that at least the *Listener* had printed my poems and stories. I destroyed my story and the two poems. I comforted myself by remembering that in my years in hospital, when I clung to my copy of Shakespeare, hiding it under straw mattresses, having it seized and scheming for its return, not often reading it but turning the tissue-paper-thin pages which somehow conveyed the words to me, I had absorbed the spirit of *The Tempest*. Even Prospero in his book-lined cell had suffered shipwreck and selfwreck; his island was unreachable except through storm.

That year I was declared officially 'sane', and in a burst of freedom following my newly acquired sanity, I accepted the invitation to stay with my sister and her husband in Northcote, Auckland. I left the Grand Hotel ('pleasant to the guests at all times') and returned to Willowglen to prepare for my Auckland journey.

18

The Photograph and the Electric Blanket

My adult life so far appeared to be a series of journeys, a dance north and south, back and forth across the country. Why did I now leave Dunedin?

Official labels carried weight: I was now officially, legally, a citizen, able to vote and make a will. Also I had decided that waitressing was not my kind of work. Up north (that magical 'up north') I would surely be able to work as a housemaid only, where I could spend my time on my own with my own thoughts, moving from room to room, making beds, dusting, polishing, without the daily conflict with the cooks in the kitchen. Also, in spite of my recurring hopes, I felt that my failure to be published in *Landfall* demanded that I take a clear view of my writing to find if my ambition were not simply and expression of 'ideas of grandeur'. Until Dr Blake Palmer had shown interest in my writing, the opinion had been that it was 'the last thing' I should do, that I should 'go out and mix and forget about writing.' The doubts came easily to the surface, and because I did not want to think about them, I planned my Auckland journey.

I brought home to Willowglen enough money to buy an electric blanket for Mother and Dad to help them through the awful winter, enough to pay for my fare and a few weeks' existence in Auckland, and to have my photograph taken at Clark's Studio in Thames Street. The photograph was urgent, a kind of reinstating of myself as a person, a proof that I did exist. In my ignorance of book publication I had supposed that all books carried photographs of their authors and I remembered my feeling, when copies of *The Lagoon* were brought to me in hospital, that I had no claim to the book, that there was not even a photograph to help stake a claim.

This, combined with my erasure in hospital, seemed to set me too readily among the dead who are no longer photographed; my years between twenty and nearing thirty having passed unrecorded as if I had never been.

I remembered how, as a child, I always stopped outside Clark's Studio, to look at the photographs behind their column of glass: they were celebrations of events in the lives of people of Oamaru who could afford to have studio photographs – there were newborn babies, infants taking their first steps, church confirmations, rows of debutantes in evening dress, club reunions, family reunions, twenty-first birthday photos, engagement and wedding photos: the complete cycle, except for the dead. There were also no photographs of resurrections.

Within the first week of my returning to Willowglen I had my hair 'washed and set' with the hairdresser assuring me that my hair would never be attractive unless it was *professionally straightened*. I looked in the top duchesse drawer where the family 'treasures' were kept, for the amber beads that Grandma gave me, but they were gone, as if I had died. Dad's medal from the War was there, and his identity disc and his soldier's paybook, and Isabel's tissue-thin *caul* which had meant, we supposed, that she would never drown.

I wore my old costume, a blouse, and no beads. The finished portrait showed a healthy young woman with obvious false teeth, a smirking smile, and a Godfrey chin. It was a fresh photo, of substance. Well, I was alive again.

I knew that the electric blanket was an attempt to give my parents more than physical warmth. I knew they wanted me to stay home and I felt guilty about leaving, as it was the tradition for the single woman to remain with her ageing parents. They were doubtful also of my ability to 'cope' in the world and, because they respected the expert opinion of the doctors, they feared that I might 'tax my brain' with writing. The electric blanket was also an attempt to bring the sunlit other world of 'down on the flat' into a house embraced most of the day by frost. I was haunted by the way mother looked out with such yearning upon the 'flat', and by her ability to weave that sun on that grass among those trees into an almost Biblical dream with fulfilment promised: some day, some day. The reminder that she was ill, that her death might not be far away, gave for me a piercing vividness to the words and gestures of those around her – my father, my brother and I – who had felt she was a gift to be cherished for ever and who could not imagine her death. Our excessive solicitude gave way at times to exasperation at her 'other-worldliness'. I felt hostile towards her because she was preparing to leave us, she was clearly tired, and her deep faith in the Second Coming of Christ and the Resurrection of the Dead, gave her an inner sense of anticipation that made her 'going down on the flat in the cool of the evening' almost a superfluous exercise. It was she who was happy merely to dream of it; I wanted its reality, just to see her relax under the pine trees in the late sun. I could see too clearly, also, the fear in my father's face when he glanced at mother: he could not bear her to leave him.

I booked my seat to Auckland. My family could not understand why I wanted to leave Willowglen, and I did not try to explain. With hopes that I might be able to have a sickness benefit while I worked at my writing, I wrote to Dr Blake Palmer whose reply shattered my hopes by its suggestion that I might 'lose the habit of working' if I were granted a benefit. The shallowness of official thinking depressed me. More depressing was the reminder that terrible treatments had been forced on me, decisions made about me, without anyone getting to know me personally; and here was just another such decision being made. My reply was to send him two poems, 'The Kite' and 'Within the Glass Mountain' where I deliberately chose imagery known to be 'schizophrenic' – glass, mirrors, reflections, the sense of being separated from the world by panels of glass – in the hope that he would get my message. I felt that there should have been some attempt by the hospital to help with resettling patients into their new lives.

I set out for Auckland, Bruddie driving me in his truck to the station. We said goodbye. Soon, I'd come home for a visit, I said. And make sure mother takes her pills.

My luggage held two copies of my new studio photograph in its mottled fawn frame.

19

Up North

Another journey. Across the Canterbury Plains and the rivers, Waitaki, peering out to find distant gum trees at Rakaia, the Rangitata; on to Lyttelton and the ferry; a calm night; then Petone, and Aunty Polly and Uncle Vere.

Aunty Polly's frog-green new car; driving around the district, pointing out General Motors where Uncle Vere worked, the Hutt River; and, proudly, the house where Bob Scott, the All Black lived.

'He lives not far from us. A local man.'

Aunty Polly was a slighter, female version of Dad – bright-eyed, quick of brain and speech, with an eye for detail and a passion for perfection. Aunty Polly was known to be 'fussy' – about her and other people's clothes, manners, ideas. She was known in our family as the aunt who had 'etiquette', and on her rare visits to our place in Oamaru her most-used sentence was 'You must have *etiquette*.' She would then list those of her family, friends and acquaintances who did not have etiquette, with highest praise given to her husband's twin sister, Gypsy. When Aunty Polly's visit to us was over, we children spent the rest of that week mimicking her in our play, 'Do you have *etiquette*, Mrs? . . . Oh, you must have *etiquette*. I've got *etiquette*!'

Mother was generous and slightly humorous in talking of Aunty Polly, 'Of course, Poll has etiquette.'

That evening I caught the train to Auckland and the next morning, shaken in all my bones, I felt the train arriving at Auckland station, and suddenly there was 'up north' again, the blue paradisal air and light.

And there were June, Wilson and their three children to meet me and drive me to their newly built house in Northcote.

Within a few days of my arrival in Auckland I found a live-in job as housemaid at the TransTasman hotel where, unlike at the Grand Hotel Dunedin with its family atmosphere, there were many rooms, many floors, a large staff, and a sense of urgency about every activity. The staff dining room was always crowded. People, unsmiling, spoke briskly, abruptly. I was given a floor to myself and the usual duties of bedmaking, room dusting and cleaning, cleaning of the corridors and bathrooms, with my own quarters a tiny room upstairs in what was called The Gods, and there should have been no problems. I soon discovered that many of the guests on my floor were pilots and passengers (from the early morning Pan American flights) who stayed in bed until late afternoon, and it was on one of these afternoons when I was still struggling with unmade beds and uncleaned rooms when I should long ago have finished, that the housekeeper discovered me and threatened to sack me if I could not work faster. I burst into tears and that evening I left the TransTasman. I had survived only one week. Auckland was a real city, a harsh city like those I had read about. I made my escape in the ferry across the harbour to gentle bushclad Northcote to stay once again with the Gordons.

I spent the next week getting to know my sister and her husband and the three children. June told me that Frank Sargeson, the writer, had visited her one day, as he had heard that I was her sister. He had said that he would like to meet me if I ever came to Auckland.

'Would you like to see him?' they asked.

'Oh no. I don't know him.'

'We can take you. He lives in an old bach at Takapuna.'

Why should I visit Frank Sargeson? I knew *Speaking for Ourselves*, and I had read some of his stories in New Zealand and English *New Writing*. I hesitated about meeting him.

Then one afternoon while they were showing me the sights of the North Shore, Wilson said suddenly, 'Frank Sargeson lives somewhere around here. Let's call on him.'

Our visit was short. What could I say? I was self-conscious, the

133

'funny' sister being taken for a drive. Mr Sargeson, a bearded old man in a shabby grey shirt and grey pants tied with string, smiled kindly and asked How I was, and I said nothing. He had an army hut vacant in his garden, he said. I was welcome to live and work there. I neither accepted nor refused, I was so overcome by my 'mental' status, and by seeing in person the famous writer whose anthology of New Zealand writing, *Speaking For Ourselves*, was a treasured book; the famous writer for whose fiftieth birthday I had signed a letter of good wishes, not knowing him and knowing nothing of the other signatories of the letter. Frank Sargeson. Mr Sargeson.

He suggested that I come to see him one day, by myself.

'How about this Friday?'

'Yes,' I said shyly.

And so on Friday I set out from Northcote towards Mr Sargeson's place in Takapuna, walking along the largely unformed road with paddocks of scrub and toi-toi on either side, past swamps of mangroves – mangroves! – and stands of native bush. It was late spring of 1954, and I'd had my thirtieth birthday, an occasion for a photograph and, in poetic tradition, for a poem. I remembered Dylan Thomas's, 'It was my thirtieth year to heaven', and I thought about his death, and tried to picture my twenties as if I had lived in the world. People were talking of watersiders, of the waterfront strike, of escaped murderers, of McCarthyism; I knew little of these. I knew only of Prospero, Caliban, King Lear, and Rilke in translation, these, for me, being occasions of the past decade.

I skirted the native bush and emerged on the road to Mr Sargeson's house, past the streets named after English poets – Tennyson Street – and was that Milton Avenue?

I arrived at Number Fourteen Esmonde Road, walked through the gap in the high hedge and around to the back door, brushing past washing hung between the lemon tree and the house. I knocked on the door.

Mr Sargeson was home. He opened the door and said, smiling nervously and speaking as if to a child, 'Come in, come in.'

I walked into the main room while Mr Sargeson went behind the wooden counter and leaned on it.

134

'You've walked a long way?'

'About three miles.'

'Would you like to lie down on the bed?'

Already apprehensive, I moved nearer the door and said primly, poised for flight, 'No thank you.'

'Robin Hyde always used to lie down. She would come limping in here and fling herself down on the bed.'

'Oh?'

'Have you read her books?'

'I've heard of them,' I said. 'I know some of her poems.'

I didn't say that I had read an essay which described her last novel as 'fantasy without ballast', the phrase staying in my mind as an example of what to expect from critics if one wrote a novel. What did it mean? Did fantasy need ballast? I felt interest in such territory because although I'd not had personal experience of inhabiting unrelieved fantasy, I had known those for whom fantasy was its own ballast. They were then free, but nowhere.

Mr Sargeson then began to talk of *The Lagoon and Other Stories* while I listened uneasily. I had not approved his choice of 'The Day of the Sheep' for the Oxford anthology.

'Do you have a copy of the Oxford anthology?' he asked. I had not. He promptly found his copy and gave it to me, signing it.

He then asked about future work.

'I don't know,' I said guardedly.

'Have you thought about coming to live and work in the hut? You'd be free to write. It's no good your living in suburbia among the nappies and bourgeois life.'

I hadn't heard anyone say the word 'bourgeois' since history lessons on the French Revolution, and I wasn't sure if I knew its modern meaning.

'I have to find a job, though,' I said.

'Why? You're a writer.'

I smiled with wonder. 'Am I? They've refused to give me a sickness benefit.'

Mr Sargeson looked angry. 'After all those years in hospital? Look, I've a good friend, a doctor who's understanding and who

135

will probably arrange a benefit for you while you work at your writing.'

'Really?'

I felt overwhelmed and shy, and protected. I accepted his offer of living and working in the hut, if he would allow me to pay him each week for my board. Although he objected at first, he finally agreed to take one pound a week. His own income was low. The first flush of publication and attention given to his work were over and he had reached the stage when he most needed money, for his books were out of print.

Both he and I were nervous that afternoon. I left saying that June and Wilson would bring me over in the weekend with my 'things' – two suitcases of clothing and books and my Remington typewriter from my days at the Grand Hotel. I felt that Mr Sargeson's offer might save my life. Already my future was bleak, with my living within a family yet feeling out of place, an extra, with my sister and her husband and family seeming like strangers to me. My sensitivity to my 'place' or lack of place and to the official judgements made about me was then extreme, and my security was shattered daily by the curious questions of the children – Who was I? Why didn't I live in my own house? Where were my children? And why wouldn't I sit with them at mealtimes? Experiences in hospital when I was once dragged by the hair to sit at the table, although I was greatly afraid of eating in the huge crowded room, watched over by the Matron and her staff, waiting for orders to make any move, and feeling the tension as the knives were collected and the long counting began – these had made me reluctant to eat in company. Usually I ate alone, thus making myself what I least wanted to seem – an oddity. Also, my sister and her husband had many friends who sometimes came to the house. I stood by, like a stone pole, while they asked politely, 'Is she better now? How is she keeping?'

I arrived at Mr Sargeson's place with my 'things', including my rust-coloured skirt, my dull green twinset and the dull green overcoat I had finally bought from Mademoiselle Modes in Dunedin. I felt bound by the rules dictated by the colour wheel and the art teaching at Training College and by the colour of my hair, to choose dull greens and browns and yellows. Primary colours, bold bright colours, were 'bad', I had been taught, while the ones I chose were supposedly 'good'. There had long been an overflow of moral judgement upon articles of clothing, colours, shapes, with the 'good' linked to 'taste', and fastened with notions of superiority.

I was sure, then, that my clothes were in 'good taste'. In my state of extreme compliance as a yes-woman, a Simon Says woman, go there, come here of course, I had even bought myself – at last – a corset or girdle, because the women at the Grand Hotel, and my sister in Auckland, had told me that my behind showed through my skirt, and in those days your behind was not at liberty to show. My only freedom was within, in my thoughts and language most of which I kept carefully concealed, except in my writing. For conversation I reserved a harmless chatter which – surely – no-one would label as 'peculiar' or 'mad'.

Once I arrived at Mr Sargeson's, however, with the prospect of living as a writer, with a place to work, to be alone, with no worry over money, and sharing meals and company with someone who actually *believed* I was a writer, the worry over colours, 'good' colours and 'bad' colours, the continued advice about my frizzy hair, and the complaint that my behind showed through my skirt, all became insignificant and far away. I had an army hut containing a bed, a built-in desk with a kerosene lamp, a rush mat on the floor, a small wardrobe with an old curtain strung in front, and a small window by the head of the bed. Mr Sargeson (I was not yet bold enough to call him Frank) had already arranged for a medical certificate and a benefit of three pounds a week which was also the amount of his income. I thus had everything I desired and needed as well as the regret of wondering why I had taken so many years to find it.

20

Mr Sargeson and the Army Hut

Mr Sargeson lived and worked to a strict routine which I adopted, although I could not change the habit of getting up in the very early morning and dressing at once. There had been no heating in the rooms of the Seacliff Brick Building, and in the early morning our bundle of clothes, outside the door during the night, was thrown in, and the air and the floor and the rusted wire netting in the small high barred window breathed frost and ice, and the caged light in the ceiling was misted over.

He did not get up until half-past seven, with breakfast at eight, and it seemed hours before I could pluck up courage to go up to the house with my chamberpot and my washing things, waiting until he was up and dressed. Usually I helped myself to my own breakfast of a yeast drink brewed overnight, home-made curds topped with honey, and bread and honey and tea. If Mr Sargeson had breakfast with me, sitting on his side of the counter, I was inclined to chatter. Within the first week of my stay he drew attention to this. 'You babble at breakfast,' he said.

I took note of what he said and in future I refrained from 'babbling', but it was not until I had been writing regularly each day that I understood the importance to each of us of forming, holding, maintaining our inner world, and how it was renewed each day on waking, how it even remained during sleep, like an animal outside the door waiting to come in; and how its form and power were protected most by surrounding silence. My hurt at being called a 'babbler' faded as I learned more of the life of a writer.

'What are you working on just now?' he asked me one day at lunch.

I was amazed and grateful at his acceptance of me as a writer doing daily work, particularly as I had not yet begun to write the novel I planned, and on some mornings I was so anxious to appear to be working that I typed The quick brown fox jumps over the lazy dog and Now is the time for all good men to come to the aid of the party; and my old favourite for unproductive moments, 'This is the forest primeval, the murmuring pines and the hemlock speak and in accents disconsolate answer the wail of the forest.'

'Oh,' I said mysteriously. 'I plan to write a novel but I'm working on other things just now.'

The 'other things' were poems and stories some of which I sent to the *Listener*, although when one, a memory of Rakaia, was returned I became reluctant to send more. Having been told that the Education Department 'paid well' for work for the school bulletins, I wrote and published two stories there. I had written a story, 'Coal', about the male patients side by side like draughthorses between the shafts of the coal cart, hauling it from ward to ward, and how, when it was decided to 'modernize' transport and a lorry was used for coal, the men who, at work between the shafts, made yet another of the sad Dickensian pictures found everywhere in the hospitals, now sat drearily in the day room, locked in with nothing to do.

I also wrote a story called 'An Electric Blanket', exploring ways of giving warmth.

'Do you have any work for me to read?'

I was taken aback. I wasn't used to showing my work to others, unless I offered it to an editor for publication. I had secret pride in my latest story, 'An Electric Blanket', and so I rashly gave it to Mr Sargeson to read.

That afternoon, instead of resting and reading in the hut, following the example of Mr Sargeson's routine, I wandered the streets of Takapuna. I sat on the beach looking out to Rangitoto, the island everyone in Auckland claimed as theirs, speaking of its perfect shape viewed from all directions as if they had helped to design and form it. 'See, there's Rangitoto,' they said. I thought, So this is the island in Charles Brasch's poem,

Harshness of gorse darkens the yellow cliff-edge,
And scarlet-flowered trees lean out to drop
Their shadows on the bay below . . .

I had little experience of many people; I knew them only in my heart; I found endearing this eagerness of Aucklanders to claim Rangitoto.

I wondered if Mr Sargeson was reading my story. Was he thinking, 'Ah, this is good, a good ending.' I was cautious in my hopes. When I read the story it swept through me and had a finality of ending, like the right chord being played. I knew, though, that it was too loosely woven; I might even have said that it sagged in the middle. Oh to have it stapled with bolts of fire to the sky!

I returned to the bach. He had been out shopping and was preparing dinner, a Spanish dish, paella, popular then as many of his friends had recently been to Spain and he liked to cook Mediterranean food. My story lay on the counter by the bunch of last year's red peppers. I took care not to fix my glance on it. Had he read it? In spite of my caution I had been sure that as soon as I came into the room he would say, 'I've read your story. It's good. Congratulations.'

Mr Sargeson poured two glasses of his favourite Lemora wine and I sat on the high wooden stool opposite him while we drank our wine.

'I read your story,' he said. He took the pages, scanned them, and read aloud, ' "Every morning she rose . . ." ' He looked sternly at me. 'Rose? Went up to heaven, I suppose? Why not say, simply, She got up. *Never* use *rose*.'

I listened contritely, realizing that 'rose' was unforgivable.

'The story is quite good of its kind,' Mr Sargeson said. I felt a surge of disappointment. I resolved not to show him more stories, and I kept my resolve, later showing him only the beginning of my novel.

'If you are working on a novel,' Mr Sargeson said, 'you must have a plan.'

He then said that he always made a list of characters. He recalled how as a child, thinking he would write a book, he had

140

begun to copy the pages of *Ivanhoe*, innocently believing he was now writing a book, when his mother found him and delivered a stern lecture on the sin of copying the work of others. He had thought that books belonged to everyone, going in and out of everyone's head, and anyone could write down any book and be a writer.

Those early months of my stay in the army hut were an unforgettable experience of sharing with Frank Sargeson (I learned to call him Frank) details of our lives, ideas and feelings, the reading of books, the evenings playing chess (which he taught me) or of my listening to the conversation between Frank and his many friends who came to dinner. Most of all we shared a working life, I learning, with his encouragement, to organize my day. I was still pursued by fears of hospital and nightmares of my experiences there. I was desperately shy, just emerging from a state of intimidation. Frank was protective and kind. I did not realize until much later when I was writing many books, how extreme but how willing his inevitable sacrifice of part of his writing life had been. I realized also that protection of others, of one person at a time, one old or ill or disabled friend, with perhaps two or three others waiting their turn in the background, was a built-in necessity of Frank's nature, side by side with his writing.

He was a skilful relentless questioner, and when I had given him details of my formal education he said, slightly disappointed, 'So you're not a primitive after all!'

He talked passionately of his early life, of his dearly loved uncle and the farm in the Waikato. He talked of his journey through Europe, showing me the collection of postcards, and in his murmured, 'I'll never see those places again. That's all over,' letting escape in his eyes and his face such a look of wild longing, almost of agony at what was gone, that I felt near to tears.

In all his conversation there was a vein of distrust, at times of hatred of women as a species distinct from men, and when he was in the mood for exploring that vein, I listened uneasily, unhappily, for I was a woman and he was speaking of my kind. I was sexually naïve, unaware, and only half awake, and I was ignorant of such subjects as homosexuality, but I felt constantly hurt by his implied

141

negation of a woman's body. My life with Frank Sargeson was for me a celibate life, a priestly life devoted to writing, in which I flourished, but because my make-up is not entirely priestly I felt the sadness of having moved from hospital where it had been thought necessary to alter the make-up of my mind, to another asylum where the desire was that my body should be of another gender. The price I paid for my stay in the army hut was the realization of the nothingness of my body. Frank talked kindly of men and of lesbian women, and I was neither male nor lesbian. He preferred me to wear slacks rather than dresses. I, who now looked on Frank Sargeson as a saviour, was forced to recognize, through the yearning sense of gloom, of fateful completeness, that the Gods had spoken, there was nothing to be done.

In exchange for this lack of self-esteem as a woman, I gained my life as I had wanted it to be. I gained also the joy of knowing a great writer, a great man, and of meeting and knowing his friends. There was always a friend 'passing through' from Wellington or the South Island or overseas, or even across the harbour from Auckland: young men with their sheaf of typewritten poems, their first harvest; old acquaintances; loved friends, male and female, young and old. Friends came and went and were talked of and gossiped about, their past, present and future, set, the gem-moments chosen skilfully, into the pattern of conversation. It was a world where appearances did not matter, where I was free at last from the ceaseless opinions about my hair and my clothes and the behind which showed through my skirt.

The time was ripe. I bought an exercise book, typing paper (green, Frank said, was easiest on the eyes), typing ribbon, and began to write my novel.

21
Talk of Treasure

Pictures of great treasure in the midst of sadness and waste haunted me and I began to think, in fiction, of a childhood, home life, hospital life, using people known to me as a base for the main characters, and inventing minor characters. For Daphne I chose a sensitive, poetic, frail person who (I hoped) would give depth to inner worlds and perhaps a clearer, at least an individual, perception of outer worlds. The other characters, similarly fictional, were used to portray aspects of my 'message' – the excessively material outlook of 'Chicks', the confusion of Toby, the earthy make-up of Francie, and the toiling parents, the nearest characters to my own parents. The setting was W, a small town which the publisher later named *Waimaru*. (Later, when the book was published, I was alarmed to find that it was believed to be autobiographical, with the characters actual members of my family, and myself the character Daphne upon whom a brain operation was performed. Confronted by a doctor who had read the book, I was obliged to demonstrate to him the absence of leucotomy scars on my temples. Not every aspiring writer has such a terrifying but convincing method of displaying to others 'proof' that she has been writing fiction. The character, Daphne, resembled me in many ways except in her frailty and absorption in fantasy to the exclusion of 'reality'; I have always been strong and practical, even commonplace in my everyday life.)

The above invasion of the 'future' is inevitable in writing autobiography particularly after one leaves childhood and the circle of being fills time and space and the lives of others, separated now from oneself and clearly visible. The process of the writing may be set down as simply as laying a main trunk railway line from Then to Now, with branch excursions into the outlying wilderness, but the real shape, the first shape is always a circle formed only to be broken and reformed, again and again.

Each day after breakfast I went to the hut to work on my novel. I had not, as Frank suggested, written a list of characters, but I had set out in my exercise book a few ideas and themes, and the names of the parts of the book which I saw as a whole before I began typing. In my exercise book I ruled lines to make a timetable with day, date, number of pages I hoped to write, number of pages written, and a space headed *Excuses*. Each day I marked the number of pages written, in red pencil.

I was ever conscious of Frank's presence and of his place in his own routine. As he had charge of the household, with a few chores to do before starting work, he began later than I, who would hear him outside in his garden rustling through the bushes to attend to his plants, the young tomatoes or peppers. Even before he began his chores he sunbathed naked against the east wall of the bach, for half an hour. He had once had tuberculosis, and he talked often of the scar and its need for oil and sunlight which, like the colour green, were beneficial to the health of the body.

Hearing the crunch and rustle of his step dangerously close to my sanctuary as he touched or snipped a straying vine of chinese gooseberry, or playfully dropped the pollen from the male flower to the female, supposing the bees or the wind had not done their work, I, who had been dreaming about my day's writing, would hurry quickly to my typewriter and begin tapping The quick brown fox jumps over the lazy dog, my ideas frozen, as always, in the presence of another person. Only when Frank went inside to begin his own work was I able to settle, typing uninterrupted until I heard the door of the bach open, footsteps rustling in the long grass, a tap on the door, and Frank's gentle voice saying, 'Are you ready for a cup of tea, Janet?' He'd put the tea on the built-in writing table, averting his gaze from the nakedness of my typed pages, then, retreating, make his way through the long grass to the bach. I'd hear the closing of the bach door. I then seized the eleven o'clock cup of tea and the rye wafer spread with honey, as if I'd been starved. Then I'd continue my work until I again heard

sounds from within the bach – Frank opening the door, fetching
the mail, scraping and clattering sounds telling of lunch being
prepared. Then promptly at one o'clock, again the rustling through
the grass, the tap on the door and the gentle voice, 'I've made
lunch, Janet.'

Eagerly, again as if I'd been starved, I hurried to the bach for
my lunch. Frank would usually have a book in his hand or on the
counter where we sat facing each other with our scrambled or
poached egg or cheese and rye bread, and he'd read extracts
aloud, and discuss the writing while I listened, accepting, believing
everything he said, full of wonder at his cleverness. I worshipped
him and was in awe of him and with my now ingrained fear of
authority or those 'in charge', I felt in need of his approval. He was
twenty years older than I, and I thought of him as an old man. I
felt trivial in mind and taste beside his rigid conscious sophistication. He informed me in a tone which said that working class
was 'good', that I was 'working class'. And once again he described
my sister and her husband, with whom I spent most weekends, as
bourgeois and once again I marvelled at the use of terms that
seemed archaic. Frank was able to place everyone within a 'class'.

After lunch he would have his 'nap', lying on the bed by the
window while I, anxious to keep to the routine, also rested or read
or wrote or perhaps walked around Takapuna. Then at three
Frank would waken and there'd be another cup of tea with a rye
wafer and honey. Then slinging his canvas bag over his shoulder
he'd go out to buy food for the evening dinner which we shared
often with friends, our most frequent visitors then being Karl and
Kay Stead who had recently married, Karl, a student at Auckland
University, and Kay a librarian. Both were in a golden glow of
youth and love and Karl was writing poetry and stories, and
both became drawn with Frank into my web of worship. Their
intelligence, their beauty, their love brought joy to Frank who was
often depressed by the general neglect of writers and by the fact
that his own books were out of print. Fairburn was said to be ill,
R. A. K. Mason was silent, and where was A. P. Gaskell? Something was sadly amiss when writers wrote one acclaimed book and
never spoke again. Speaking for Ourselves, indeed! The message

of silence was too depressing. Also, Frank felt subdued by my apparent ease of writing: he was not to know how often I was forced to make the quick brown fox jump over the lazy dog, all good men to come to the party, and to sit brooding in the 'forest primeval' while the 'murmuring pines and the hemlock' spoke and 'in accents disconsolate answered the wail of the forest.'

The friendship of Karl and Kay filled my life giving me at last a place in my own years, for I felt I had lost so many years that I could not determine my 'real' age. I felt old beside the youth of Karl and Kay, and young beside Frank. I was not yet thirty-one.

My writing was accompanied by reading: I had many books to read.

'Have you read Proust?' Frank asked.

'No.'

When he was excited or nervous he had a habit of suddenly moving his arms and legs as if he were dancing. Now, he 'danced' with the excitement of introducing *Proust* to my life. I was completely ignorant, even pronouncing the name incorrectly, although I remembered a remark of someone in Dunedin, 'It's like a scene from Proust.'

Dutifully at first, but inspired by Frank's enthusiasm, I began to read Proust, in the evening by the light of the kerosene lamp in the hut, the shadow of the flame wavering across the page. Entangled by the simplicity of the first sentence, 'For a long time I used to go to bed early,' I was soon trapped in Proust's world and each day Frank and I talked of the highlights of what I had read.

'And of course you've read *War and Peace*.'

I had not.

'It's time I re-read War and Peace,' Frank said, and once again I was impressed by his organization of his life as a writer (remembering that he was perhaps the first professional writer living in New Zealand, an apprentice of ghosts in a world of distance). An accountant would say, I must study those old columns of figures. A writer re-reads the classics, sweeping away present trivia, renewing inspiration, and marvelling at the imperishable truth and beauty; perhaps not every writer; but this was Frank's way.

As he had lately had a copy of *War and Peace* from Roy Parsons who supplied him with books he couldn't afford to buy, often in exchange for reviews for *Parsons Packet*, he lent this copy to me while he re-read his original copy, with larger print. Frank was always aware that his eyes were precious, and as with the oil and the sunlight for his scar, he sought substances that were 'good for the eyes': carrots, certainly. Green typing paper and green shades on the lamps. He also wore an eyeshade, like that worn by tennis players. At his suggestion I too bought myself an eyeshade.

Together we lived through the events of *War and Peace*, Frank showing excited pleasure at my page by page discoveries which we talking of together, analyzing the characters, their actions and feelings, and every day at lunch he would say eagerly, 'Where are you now?'

When we had finished *War and Peace* we read *Anna Karenina, Resurrection*, and the stories. Tolstoy inhabited Number Fourteen Esmonde Road, Takapuna, Auckland – both the bach and the dilapidated army hut. The characters lived there – in the room with the corner bed with its sagging mattress and threadbare blankets; with the high shelves of books, the rolled and tied faded manuscripts along the top shelf; the fireplace with the manuka logs stacked ready for the evening fire; the collection of postcards, letters, small sculptures on the mantelpiece; with the paintings on the wall – *the sugar barge at Chelsea*; with the built-in table between the bookshelves, once used as a desk but now piled with yellowing copies of the *Times Literary Supplement*, the *New Statesman*, and other journals, the electric light above shaded with its square of green cloth faded white around the edges; the room with the worn unpainted counter where we ate our meals, with the cupboards and sink and the hotwater cupboard where the curds warmed for the next morning's breakfast; the small Atlas stove in the corner; the army-style tin kitchen utensils, the one or two or three white cups, two without handles; the huge wooden wireless built, Frank said, by 'Bob Gilbert' which Frank discreetly switched on when he used the lavatory in the small adjacent bathroom (he was a modest man, secretive; but his jokes were brilliantly lewd).

All Tolstoy's characters lived, and some died in that room with its windows open to the honeysuckled front hedge, and, at evening, the windows shaded by placing a row of painted canvases against the glass; but the night sky always looked in, and for months the cicadas sang all day and the crickets sang all night.

The mosquitoes sang too, swarming from the mangrove swamp at the end of the road.

We saved *The Death of Ivan Ilych* for our last reading. Frank was shocked when he learned that I had never read it.

'The great classic,' he said.

I took the small dark blue book with its silken place-thread to the hut to read, and the next evening we talked of Ivan Ilych and of death.

There is a freedom born from the acknowledgement of greatness in literature, as if one gave away what one desired to keep, and in giving, there is a new space cleared for growth, an onrush of a new season beneath a secret sun. Acknowledging any great work of art is like being in love; one walks on air; any decline, destruction, death are within, not in the beloved; it is a falling in love with immortality, a freedom, a flight in paradise.

I cannot help remembering with love my days at Esmonde Road. There is the immediacy of sitting on my high stool facing Frank across the counter as we talked of *War and Peace*, and as we talk we are no longer in Esmonde Road, we are with Pierre, gone to see the War and looking on the face of Napoleon; or we are beside the stubborn slowly budding oak, the last to comply with the seasons, the last to give up its leaves; or at the deathbed of the old Prince, he, too, stubborn as an oak, in conflict with the season.

We also read Olive Schreiner's *Story of An African Farm*, becoming so steeped in it that we became Waldo and Bonaparte Blenkins. If Frank could not transform me into a male companion at least he could give me a boy's name: Waldo.

Among my possessions was my radiogram from my days at the Grand Hotel, and my record of Beethoven's Seventh Symphony. I sensed at once Frank's disapproval of this 'luxury' item; 'If you need music, carry it in your head or listen to it first hand.' The radio was an 'excused' item. I adopted Frank's belief that radiograms, cameras, tape recorders were unnecessary, even *bourgeois*, and, ashamed, I hid my radiogram in the wardrobe under an old skirt. One evening however, when Karl and Kay brought two records, A Little Night Music and Beethoven's Violin Concerto played by David Oistrach, Frank said, 'We can play them on Janet's radiogram.' Accepting it. I can still see that room with the bare wallboard and the wooden floor which Frank oiled each Saturday morning with a mop soaked in linseed oil ('it keeps down the dust'), with the canvas chairs ('the most comfortable type') with their wooden arms, the room that already held all the characters from *War and Peace*, *Anna Karenina*, the stories of Tolstoy and Chekhov, from Proust, Flaubert, Olive Schreiner, Doris Lessing, receiving now the music of Mozart and Beethoven while we listen. We play the record again. Karl and Frank begin to talk about Yeats. Karl reads 'Sailing to Byzantium', 'The Circus Animals' Desertion'. While I, bred on the 'old' Yeats, that is, the 'young' Yeats, of 'Had I the heavens' embroidered cloths' and 'The Lake Isle of Innisfree', listen, bathed in the words and the music. I think that I recite, then, the poem I knew by heart, Dylan Thomas's 'After the Funeral', and we talk of the meaning of 'the strutting fern lay seeds on the black sill'.

That evening I read in bed by the light of the kerosene lamp, Frank's copy of the *Poems* of Yeats:

> We had fed the heart on fantasies,
> The heart's grown brutal from the farc;
> More substance in our enmities
> Than in our love; O honey-bees,
> Come build in the empty house of the stare.

I finished *Talk of Treasure* two weeks before my thirty-first birthday, and taking my typescript, newly bound with tape in the way Frank had shown me, and a copy of William Faulkner's *A Fable* which I had promised to review for *Parsons Packet*, I travelled home for two weeks to Oamaru and Willowglen.

22

The Pine Trees in the Cool of the Evening

The South Island was more reluctantly awakening to spring; frost lay on the grass; there was talk of snow and fear for the newborn lambs in the high country; the daily newspapers needed more space to record the usual winter toll of loved grandparents. At Willowglen the old lichen-covered trees in the orchard showed buds fattening into blossom, the may tree was already white and the wattle displayed its gold down by the tenantless fowlhouse.

Many-kittened Siggie greeted me with a baby rabbit which at once sprang away unharmed into the next-door paddock. I found Siggie's Matilda, the once-kitten on which Isabel and I had practised our newly-discovered psychology, defining her 'inferiority complex', lying dead, stiff and frosted under the bee-swarming flowering currant bush – for, as always on arriving at Willowglen, I explored 'outside' first, clambering up the bank at the back of the house among years of fallen composted pear-tree leaves and fruit that stuck to the soles of my shoes and sent me skating down the dampened path. I explored the creek and the swamp and the daffodils in flower under the orchard trees, and I walked under the pine trees 'down on the flat' touching and smelling the blobs of sap-like pine-tree pearls glued to the trunks of the trees. The circumstances of our shifting from 56 Eden Street when we were 'turned out' of what I'd always believed was our home, and the anxiety of the time of the search for a 'place' made Willowglen the equivalent of paradise, and it, not being human, was able to receive all the love heaped upon it, and survive and blossom.

I knew I was only a fair-weather visitor, that I could not bear to be reminded that the family season was winter, no matter how many fruit trees and flowers blossomed outside. Mother had lost weight and was clearly failing in health while at the same time denying her condition. As ever she was full of hope, and her immediate delight was her success in persuading a clump of chives to grow in the small herb garden she had planted just outside the lean-to in the rich pear-composted soil. Although her inner life was full of sustaining joys and surprises, she expressed so few personal wishes and these were so seldom granted, that the clump of chives was an event in her life with her moving gently and happily to the next phase of bliss, a 'chive sandwich with fresh bread and plenty of butter.' Faced with the prospect of her death, and now with her unusual action to grant herself a personal wish, my father, with fear in his eyes, turned to his refuge of mockery, 'Mum and her chives, just look at her!' I always knew that the 'outward' Dad was not the 'inward' Dad, and I felt pity for his inability to ally feelings with the right words instead of with words and actions seized in panic from an outer space of being human. There was such waste in his continued mockery.

My father had taught his children well. I too resented the inevitability of mother's death. I felt helpless and hopeless and I spoke sternly to her, pleading with her to take her pills, to rest, to cease her everlasting fuelling of fires and cooking and caring, and come 'down on the flat in the cool of the evening in the last rays of the sun' as she dreamed of doing. Although I was a competent cook, having remembered the cooking lessons of Junior High days, and experimented since when I had the chance, mother's confidence was undone if another person cooked the meals or baked the cakes. (She still suffered from the reference to her as 'a bad household manager'.) If I baked bread or small cakes or cooked one of my 'specialities', mother immediately baked 'her' bread, 'her' cakes, and 'her' speciality, attempting a kitchen counterpart so transparent in meaning that I found it endearing and depressing, and withdrew my own floury melody.

During my stay I read to mother selected pages from *Talk of Treasure*, naturally leaving out all reference to the death of the mother, Amy Withers. I read only the 'harmless, happy' paragraphs while mother said faithfully, 'That's lovely.' She, and Dad, were more interested in 'this Mr Sargeson', but they appeared to be satisfied when I explained, 'He's an old man, a famous writer.' My parents had given up hope that their daughter, who had been years in a mental hospital, would 'meet her fate', but people visiting, often said slyly to me, 'Have you met your fate, yet?' It seemed to me an old-fashioned, even a Victorian expression.

I spent time with Dad, too, down on the wharf fishing, and I was as amazed and grateful as I had been when I was a child and we had shared the crosswords and the detective stories, when he began to tell stories remembered from his childhood, of seafaring characters in Oamaru. It was cold down on the wharf with the sea wind. The green milky-murky waves lapped and sucked at the old wooden piles on the inner side of the harbour where Dad waited for the cod to bite, while I sat facing north, the open sea, where the water was a clear stony grey lapping on rocks. We caught dogfish and a ling which we used for bait to catch the blue cod. I really didn't care about fishing, but the chances to be with my father were rare. He fished in silence; we talked only when we had a catch to deal with.

'Never eat red cod,' he said, when I showed him the red cod on the end of my line. 'They're full of worms. The blue cod are the ones to keep.'

I listened obediently, wonderingly as if I were being taught by a great teacher, while, always aware of a life of writing, I stored his words at the back of my mind for future use.

And while I was at Willowglen, in the midst of other activities, I was reading *A Fable* and other William Faulkner novels from the library. Spinning, spinning, awhirl, where am I? That might describe my feeling on reading the first page of William Faulkner. I read on and on, I read through the book, and when I had finished I was still awhirl in pools of words and feeling which affected me like powerful music where the meaning is seldom questioned. I was preparing a review – how could I write a review of a novelist who clouded my vision with feeling? I returned to the book, reading it again and again, slowly emerging into the clear fountain-light where the characters, the scenes, the meaning appeared starkly outlined, solid, real, good. This was William Faulkner's world, and I had found it to keep.

152

A few days before I caught the train to the north, I persuaded mother to picnic with me 'on the flat', and so, late one afternoon, we made chive sandwiches and filled a thermos with tea; and carrying a rug and cushions we set out for 'the flat', walking slowly down the path beneath the old 'ghost' pine tree, past the old apple shed where the fantails danced in and out of the broken-hinged open door, past the cowbyre with its roof of sky and broken bail, the rotted pigsty where Siggie went regularly to have her kittens, by the old stables where furniture, pictures, boxes of photographs, most of the relics of 56 Eden Street were stored, thrust without order on that wild, disorderly day of the shift; through the gate out of the cool shadow of the hill, at last where the stripling pines lay in the warm sun shining like another sun, not *our* sun, in another place. We spread the rug on the pine needles and leaned against the trees, the sticky resin clinging to our clothes. Feeling the warmth of the sun, I wriggled like a lizard come out to bask. We ate our sandwiches of bread and butter and chives and drank with little black flies from the creek dropping in the tea. The pukekos watched us through the fence in the next paddock.

But mother was restless. What if the phone rang? Surely we wouldn't hear it, down on the flat? What if 'your father' came home and found no dinner prepared? Besides, she had meant to phone the weekly order at the grocer's, the Self Help, and it might be too late for the order-boy to deliver it. We had moved our patronage from the Star Stores to the Self Help when the son of one of our Eden Street neighbours became manager. Having lived in Oamaru for many years, my family now had a faithful network of favourite shopkeepers, post office clerks, taxi drivers, many of whom were the 'boys' who used to dream, with Myrtle and me, of making the big-time in Hollywood. Some of those who dreamed with us were now bones in the Western Desert, in Crete, or Italy.

Our picnic was too soon over. Mother struggled to her feet, breathless with the effort, and together we climbed the path up to the house; and already the sun had gone down on the flat, the driveway was growing dark, darkened more quickly by the presence of the pine trees, and we were once again where the frostbound

153

hill leaned over the house, gripping it with a claw of everlasting winter.

Two days later when I boarded the express for the north I knew I would not see mother again, and in a burst of bitterness I said, 'I'm never coming back to Willowglen.'

My words hurt, as I knew they would. I said goodbye and the train pulled out on its familiar track, and even as it began its *Kaitangata, Kaitangata, Kaitangata, Winton, Winton, Winton, Kakanui, Kakanui, Kakanui*, I knew there was no use escaping anywhere, from family or frost or land, the escape made impossible anyway because, as the daughter of a railway worker, I had to accept the possession of and by every inch of railway track in the country: an iron bond of mutual ownership. The train continued to say a new word, *Willowglen, Willowglen, Willowglen*, as we crossed the Canterbury Plains.

23

A Death

Willowglen may have been the paradise of leaves, earth, dark water, swamps thick with green-for-danger bright grasses, but Auckland was still the paradise of light, full of swirling smoky clouds as if a volcano hid in the sky, erupting to another unseen world. Frank's garden was bursting with the spring plantings – tall columns of sweet corn growing outside the hut window, peppers shiny greenleaved on the east side of the house. He was planting Russian Red tomatoes, and he showed me the picture on the empty seed packet.

'Beefsteak and Russian Red, that's what I'm planting this year.'

There was a tiny pawpaw tree, too, near the hut. He nursed it carefully. He hoped one day to grow a custard apple. Barbara and Maurice Duggan, he said, had grown a custard apple. 'Perhaps the only one in the country.'

His wonder was endless; his eyes glistened when he talked of the custard apple (I was about to say 'his eyes *shone*', but the light in them was not a steady planetary shining, it was broken light coming through mist or dampness or plain tears).

'But what about your manuscript?' he asked. 'Have you sent it to Pegasus?'

When Denis Glover left the Caxton Press he apparently gave a handful of my stories and poems to Albion Wright of Pegasus who sent them on to me. I prompted burned them. Among the papers was a letter from John Forrest to Denis Glover explaining that there was no hope for my recovery ('when I think of you I think of Van Gogh, of Hugo Wolf . . .'). Frank explained that Pegasus had taken over much of the Caxton Press's work.

I knew that after the cool reception of my story 'An Electric

Blanket', I could not show Frank any of the book. I read, however, a token few lines from the beginning which Frank liked so much that he suggested I send it as a poem to John Lehmann of the *London Magazine*. To make matters more interesting (we had been talking about the Australian Hoax of *Angry Penguins and Ern Malley*) Frank suggested I collect a few poems I had written, and he would send them to John Lehmann. He chose a name for me – *Sante Cruz* – repeating solemnly as if I did not know, 'That means *Saint* and *Cross*.' His letter to John Lehmann explained that I was a woman from the Pacific Islands who was new to Auckland; he had been impressed with my writing. The reply was kind. The poems, John Lehmann said, were refreshing, new; he hoped that when I learned a little more English he might see more of my work.

In the meantime Frank helped me parcel the manuscript, and such was his care for it that he insisted on walking with me to the post office and watching while the clerk stuck on the correct stamps and thrust the envelope into the chute.

Two weeks later I heard that Pegasus Press had accepted my book. They enclosed a contract to be signed. I was bewildered, pleased, and scared, while Frank, having learned the routine of writing and publishing, and knowing the *etiquette*, said, 'We must celebrate.' Spending more than he could afford he bought a bottle of Vat 69 whisky which we drank that evening.

Summer came too quickly. The heat persisted day and night. I slept with the door of the hut open, the entry and the window by my bed, draped with muslin to keep out mosquitoes from the mangrove swamp and from Lake Pupuke. Having finished my book and being thrust once again into the ordinary factual world, I grew restless, unable to work in the heat. I wrote poems, a few stories. I played chess in the evenings or again listened to the anecdotes and conversation of Frank and his friends, or he and I talked over the books we were reading, but we both knew there had been a subtle change of emotional gear, we were no longer on the same path, the honeymoon was over. I knew it would soon be time to leave and I did not want to leave. Beginning, middle, end – how often we had talked of the fictional processes and how each could be expressed painlessly, invisibly.

Then one day early in December my sister and her husband came unexpectedly to see me. It was morning, working time. I heard Frank direct them to the hut.

June appeared at the door.

'I came to tell you,' she said. 'Mother died this morning. She had a stroke at about six o'clock and she died at half-past ten. Bruddie rang to tell Wilson and me.'

I tried to show as little feeling as possible. I said, 'She was worn out, anyway, and she was ready to die.'

On the deaths of Myrtle and Isabel we had embraced each other and cried, but that had been so long ago and I'd been on my own, alone with my feelings, for so many years.

'Her life was awful,' I said.

June agreed. They were not going to the funeral, she said. She asked would I be coming over as usual for the weekend.

'No, I don't think so,' I said.

'We'll see you some time then?'

'Yes.'

'They didn't want to worry you with the news, they told us to tell you.'

The mixture of sadness and relief at mother's death was strengthened and sharpened by my familiar feeling of anger and depression at being treated as the 'frail, mad' member of the family who must be sheltered from unpleasant news. The well-meaning consideration of my family served to emphasize and increase my separation from them. I was jealous of my sister's first knowledge of the death, almost as if it were a treasured gift chosen to be given to her, then passed on, used and soiled, secondhand, to me. It was partly a reawakening of the former childhood rivalries in being first to know, to see, the first to embrace the cherished secret; in fact, the rivalry had never reawakened for it had never slept!

I told Frank my news.

'So what?' he said, showing his bitterness towards his own family. 'Parents are better dead.'

Bravely, I agreed with him.

That night in the privacy of the hut I wept, and the next morning, faced with Frank's scornful reproaches about 'all those tears', I explained that I was weeping for mother's life, not for her death. I regretted that with our parents' lives spent almost entirely in feeding, clothing, sheltering us, we had little time to know and be friends with them. My life had been spent watching, listening to my parents, trying to decipher their code, always searching for clues. They were the two trees between us and the wind, sea, snow; but that was in childhood. I felt that their death might expose us but it would also let the light in from all directions, and we would know the reality instead of the rumour of wind, sea, snow, and be able to perceive all moments of being.

I stayed the weekend at the hut, and so on Sunday I shared the meal that Frank always cooked for his friend Harry, while Harry, at first silent as a speaking plank of wood, soon lost his suspicion of me and talked to me while Frank, more nervous than usual and showing it by the excessive gesturing and waving of his hands, stirred and tasted and measured and dipped and finally served his usual perfect meal. After the meal I returned to the hut leaving Frank and Harry to talk over old and new times. They had known each other so long that they used half-sentences or single words for conversation, and when I came to know Harry a little I realized how much Frank prized him, not only as a lasting companion, but as a source of information about the 'other' world of racecourses and sleazy city hotels and sad derelict wanderers down by the Ferry Buildings and lower Queen Street. Frank had staged his own life perfectly, with himself as a writer, and he made sure that while he lived within the act of writing he was surrounded by characters who would bring him news from the world he could no longer explore in reality when the physical demands of fiction mean a seat at a desk or table, all morning or all day, and silence, solitude, and sleep.

No-one expected me to go to mother's funeral; I fulfilled my family's expectations of me by not feeling able to go. Instead, I asked my father to send me the letters and telegrams of sympathy which I answered. Then I celebrated and mourned mother in a handful of poems. Their movement is not good but they do give details of what I was thinking.

Burn the dirty clothes she died in,
the sour stockings, the stained dress,
the holey (holy) interlock
she wore to greet the sad surprise
the sad morning surprise of death.

Put her costume on a hanger
on the clothes-line for the wind
to blow the shreds of sick disaster
into the trees or the next town.
Lay the death-sheets on the lawn
for dew and sun to bleach and clean.

I say that only fire and air
are kindly charities, so give
to them your pennyworth of grief
refusing earth and water who buried
her body, drowned her with too many tears.

Another poem –

Whose death will never kill its moment, smoke out
from her heart the small dire ferret of time
will not walk again, her heavy body in garment
outsize, sunflower hat; in seven-league shoes
across bog, byre-mud, snowgrass after her runaway
rabbit of God who bred deep, his warren
burrowed secret from the hawk beneath her paddock
of stone and thistle, flaglily and bracken.

Though my chisel of salt will not cut or reshape
her stone, my tears increase no flight of thistledown
or tell its time of travel, though night flay her lilies,
her blue bog-sunrise, her palpitating Gods
breed in darkness, still let the crazed hawk refugees
fly down to her bed of bracken, sleep safe.

What else could I write, having the examples of George Barker's,
'Most near most dear most loved and most far,' and 'After the
funeral, mules' praises, brays . . .' by Dylan Thomas?

My preoccupation then was with condensed imagery and the
use of general terms – love, death, charity, heart – which are like
small grenades set within a poem – the feeling, touching them,

explodes itself into powerless fragments and so at the end of the poem the feeling has either been destroyed or dispersed, and nothing remains. The condensed imagery also has the effect of jet travel – you see nothing of the landscape beneath and thus are unaffected by it, and when you arrive at your destination – or the end of the poem – you are as fresh – apart from the tedium of travelling – as when you set out, and the poem might as well be nothing, a shadow.

Trying to write poetry, I did my best, although I knew the poems were not 'good'. I spent much feeling (which might better have been used in strengthening the poems) in hoping they were good while knowing they were not – the ice cream indulgence of a dream.

I wrote one other poem about mother's death, 'Their eyes pleading the light are mocked by light' which I read to Karl Stead, and although he was years younger than I and had written less poetry, his judgement and sense of rightness were keener than mine. He listened and said little, but when he repeated the words, frowning, 'The sun is death's lawyer,' I knew the poem was a failure because I then had the urge to say, like one caught in the misdemeanour of a poem, 'Oh, I can explain everything.'

I could, too. The metaphor was worked out, but it did not strike.

> Their eyes pleading the light are mocked by light
> if scribbled nought beyond, within, themselves –
> the doom or flame-encircling litigant
> paid by decay to prosecute their lives;
> for now in magnitude of mourning, relatives
> beachcombing, probe my mother's body,
> gull through binoculars of fear and grief
> above the coast to seek her hieroglyph,
> where death's most ardent lawyer, the sun
> of December, in this her sixty-third year
> has wakened early for darkest work, has written
> client signatures across her skin
> like tributaries dry without cipher
> bedded on bone, on gaunt and decaying bone
> misled, tongueless, to the tasting-edge
> of her stopped blood – this, who could have foreseen?

I was strongly affected by the fact that mother died in the morning, the work-time, that she had got up (never 'risen') early, and gone to the kitchen and had lit the fire and when Dad found her she, half-conscious, whispered to him, 'I thought I'd make a cup of tea . . .' These were her last words; she never regained consciousness. As a statement of her life they could be judged, without cynicism, as her best literary effort.

My continued feeling of betrayal that Frank had shown no sympathy at mother's death, melted when I overheard him say to Kathleen, our neighbour, 'A mother's death is hardest to take. It's a sad time for Janet.' Frank, too, had secret feelings to hide!

24
The Silkworms

When the summer is over, I thought, and the weather is cooler (a dream: in the cool of the evening) I shall write another novel. Emerged from my fictional world I can see clearly that my staying in the hut was using more of Frank's time, energy and feeling than he had bargained for, as I was not his only *charge* (the word in all its variety of meaning), and each (Harry, Jack, old Jim next door, Frank's two elderly aunts, one of whom was blind, who lived near the beach in an old gabled house full of high dark furniture) had to be visited and listened to and comforted, with the poorer 'charges' receiving vegetables from the garden, or a ten shilling or pound note. The visit to the aunts most consumed Frank's energy, for their tongues were sharply critical while he remained patiently docile. When he returned from seeing them, he always said, in a tone of amazement, *'My fat aunts, my huge aunts.'* And they were huge aunts with a kind of solidity that would seem to be incapable of ever melting: I think they were Frank's mother's sisters; and I think they were like the past, his past, in being unable to vanish: they were not snow-women; they were without season or time; and when the sick blind aunt lay in bed, one day when I visited with Frank, she was diminished not by her blindness or sickness but only by the tall oak bookcase that loomed by the bed.

The heat of the summer persisted. Frank began to talk of the 'golden time' in his childhood when he kept silkworms. It was a remembered summer, like 'That Summer' of his short perfect novel. It happened then that one day I was walking in Karangahape Road (a 'possession' of Auckland, like Rangitoto) when I noticed silkworms displayed in a pet-shop window. I bought half a dozen and that evening I nervously unwrapped them and set them on the kitchen counter. The sensitivity between Frank and myself was now so extreme that every movement had to be planned for fear of hurting or implying by one a state which could not be borne in the other. I had seen Frank come near to weeping over his postcards of his early European journey; I felt that the golden time of his uncle and the silkworms belonged only to him, and I did not want him to think that I, listening to his constant remembering of a childhood happiness, had dared to try to provide him with a replica of the past. I was casual about the silkworms. He was delighted with an immediate, not a recollective delight. He, in his turn, viewed the silkworms as a means of absorbing *my* attention while he and I planned my next 'move' which, according to Frank, was for me to 'travel overseas' to 'broaden my experience', a convenient way, both he and I realized, of saying that I was 'better out of New Zealand before someone decided I should be in a mental hospital.' We both knew that in a comformist society there are a surprising number of 'deciders' upon the lives and fate of others. Frank even suggested that he become my next of kin in a marriage of convenience which I then found insulting, and he, on overnight reflection, decided against.

We concentrated on the silkworms, I roaming the neighbourhood of Takapuna until I found in an old-fashioned garden overlooking the beach and the pohutukawa trees, the mulberry tree with leaves to feed our 'charges', and a kindly owner willing to give me supplies of leaves. Frank brought home a shoebox from Hannahs shoe store, nestled the mulberry leaves inside and gently lay the silkworms upon the leaves. At once they began to eat. During the day we kept the box on the end of the counter near the bookcase, and at night I took it down to the hut and set it on my desk-table. We knew the silkworms were eating for *dear life*. In the silence of the night as I lay in bed I heard a sound like the turning of tiny pages in a tiny library, which I've heard only since then, slightly magnified, in the library of the British Museum as the readers steadily consume page after cherished page of their chosen books. The silkworms' consuming was literal, the sound of steady chewing and chomping all night and all day, although unlistened to during the day, without pause until that stage of their life was over: a lifelong meal. Frank explained what would happen next, and we watched as the silkworms entered their next life, as they began to wave their heads in a circular motion, with a thread like the golden spiderweb being drawn from their mouths. Frank had placed each on a strip of cardboard which they used as their anchorage, enclosing themselves and the cardboard in a golden cocoon, and when all was still within, Frank gently cut through the silk, removing the naked grubs and wrapping them in nests of cotton-wool – the usual intrusion based on the belief that we own the world, its creatures and its produce. The golden thread of plaited silk hung on the wall by the window in that same room where Ivan Ilych and the old Prince died, and Pierre saw Napoleon, and the oak tree budded and shed its leaves, and Mozart and Beethoven had their music played: a rich gold room.

In time, the grubs, cosy in their cottonwool, became moths which in their first moments sought each other, male and female, the males mounting the females for mating that lasted, like the eating and spinning, all day and night, until the males fell torpid, dying one by one, while the females again with their furniture provided, laid tiny rows of white eggs, like Braille dots or stitches, neatly upon the sheet of cardboard; then they also died whereupon Frank who in all the stages of the silkworms' development had repeated his actions of years ago, explaining each stage, describing how it would be, set the sheet of cardboard with the silkworms enclosed in their own past, present and future, in the shoebox, which he buried, lowering it like a makeshift coffin into the earth.

'That's the cycle,' he said, his words and his glance capturing other references, other species.

'They'll stay there in the winter, and when the warm weather comes, I'll dig them up, they'll hatch, and the cycle will repeat itself.'

The completeness, perfection, and near indestructibility of the cycle did not escape us.

That evening, like Gods, we celebrated with Vat 69 the lives dedicated to eating, spinning, mating.

The next day we planned a letter to the Literary Fund applying for a grant for me to 'travel overseas and broaden my experience.' I was now free to accept the invitation from one of Frank's friends, Paula Lincoln, known as P. T. Lincoln, or Paul, to stay at her bach at Mount Maunganui while we awaited the outcome of my application.

25

Miss Lincoln, Beatrix Potter and Dr Donne

I had met Paula Lincoln when she once visited Frank, and I had seen her as a small grey-haired woman with a voice full of tears as she talked of how her body had 'changed' and of how she had been deprived of her share of peace. She was in distress that afternoon. I could see Frank's movement away from her as he, disliking displays of feeling, tried to escape the fountain of inexplicable misery where she seemed to be the central figure, the statue, receiving all.

If only, I thought, she didn't go on so.

I could sense that her past and Frank's were bound up in her feelings. I never solved the mystery of that afternoon. When she had gone Frank murmured sadly without explaining, 'Poor woman. She gets in a state. Every time she comes here she's in a state. By the way, she has invited you to stay at the Mount whenever you feel like a holiday. Poor woman. I'm very fond of her.'

He showed me a photo of a young Frank with three friends, one a small pretty dark-haired woman. 'That's her. Paul.'

He explained about her life, how she had been educated at a famous public school for girls, how she had broken away from her 'upper class' family to come to New Zealand when she was thirty, and how she had worked as a physiotherapist, and during the War, with the Pacifist Council; how she readily became interested in causes, how they had met, she became interested in writing, how a small inheritance gave her a private income with freedom to write, but she had written only a few stories. She had helped Frank with money for the building of his bach and the publishing of his first book.

I said that I remembered her story in *Speaking for Ourselves*.

166

'She's a wonderful person,' Frank said. 'She's a lesbian, you know.'

Even with my growing knowledge of the varieties of sexual preference, I was unaware of the meaning and implication of lesbianism, and when Frank explained it to me, I found that I, like Queen Victoria, didn't believe it!

I set out for Mount Maunganui. The train journey lasted most of the day and was one of a number of train routes then where the journey took so long and was so much a part of the natural surroundings of bush, waterfalls, ferns, wet clay, a glistening world of wet, that the heart of the land entered the railway carriage and there was the feeling of the loneliness and strangeness of a personal exploration. There were few passengers, some lying sleeping on the seats, others like myself sitting alone in a double-seat, all a prey to the wild world beyond the carriage windows. Once when the train was forced to a stop before a landslide of clay covering the line, the driver and fireman and a trolley of gangers worked with shovels clearing the line while the passengers sat silently immersed in the green dream, and when the train at last began to move, creaking slowly around narrow bend after narrow bend where rainwater oozed from every pore of earth and bark and leaf and fern, there was the privilege of knowing, like being favoured with a secret, that this was not the 'main trunk line', accepted by use, with refreshment stops and cities along the way, this was a 'branch line' with all its mystery, neglect, vague atmosphere of exile which is the nature of branch lines everywhere, even in dreams, thinking, and history.

Finally the train stopped at Tauranga, and although it was to continue along the isthmus towards Mount Maunganui, Paula Lincoln had arranged to meet me in Tauranga so that we might take the evening launch across the harbour. It was already dark with a wintry full moon. Paula Lincoln was waiting on the platform, dressed as she had been the day she visited Frank – grey flannel slacks, white cotton blouse like a school blouse, grey cardigan, and gaberdine raincoat. Her shoes were black lace-up 'sensible' winter shoes. She was eager and nervous, speaking in the English accent which we used to call 'Oxford', heard in teachers, doctors and

167

royalty which therefore gave it an association with authority, a hint of admonishment. P. T. L.'s voice had a defensive note as if holding a permanent thread of *This is why it is so and it can't be helped.*

We walked from the station to the jetty, with Miss Lincoln bright-eyed, steeped now not in a fountain of misery but in the moonspray and moonlight, for suddenly the clouded sky cleared and the light poured down on the harbour. Even the silkworms had consumed time with their mulberry leaves: the cold of the night was winter, May, cold.

We boarded the launch, and as we moved on to the expanse of harbour, Miss Lincoln trailed her hand over the side, touching the water, and murmuring, 'liquid lumps of light'.

'That's how Greville described it,' she said. 'Has Frank talked about Greville Texidor? Have you read her stories?'

I said I had seen *These Dark Glasses*, Greville's stories. I had been impressed and quietly depressed by their assurance and sophistication. Frank had talked, too, of Greville and her life, giving the condensed biography that accompanied talk of each of his friends and acquaintances, and stressing the personal marvel of nature, talent or experience that each held like a dazzling lure: Greville's was the fact that she had once been married to a contortionist and had toured the world with him. *'Very early in her life.'* Frank admired her writing, too, but it was her 'experience of life' that captured him: where she had been, what she had been, what she had seen, and what she had done – with her contortionist husband!

As the launch neared the Mount, Miss Lincoln continued to talk of Greville and of Frank and his early life with his friends. Then we were silent, enjoying the moonlight, and when the launch pulled in to the jetty, Miss Lincoln said, 'I like to be with someone and not have to talk all the time.'

'Oh, so do I,' I said with new-acquaintance enthusiasm. Frank had told me that Paul didn't 'take to' people easily. 'She'll like you,' he said. 'You'll be good for each other.'

Frank sometimes dispensed people as if they were medicine and he were the doctor in charge of the case. He prescribed for

168

himself, too. Cooking Sunday dinner for Harry and hearing him talk about his world of horseracing, and listening to Jack's woes and dreams, and looking after Jim next door were seen by Frank as being, among the pleasures, 'good for him'. I was wondering what would happen if Frank's friend, Miss Lincoln, didn't 'take to' me, or, in her language which held a number of words used in school stories and in Somerset Maugham, if we didn't 'click'.

'Everyone calls me Paul,' she said, as we walked towards the beach road. 'I've been Paul since my school days.' (I had been mumbling at intervals, 'Miss Lincoln'.)

'Well . . .' I said.

Mount Maunganui was like a sandy settlement in the middle of the sea, with the sea as the only horizon, and as we walked past the cluster of beach stores where Miss Lincoln stopped to buy bread and fruit, we came suddenly into Ocean Beach Road.

> Round the cape of a sudden came the sea
> And the moon looked over the mountain's rim

we quoted together.

'I always think of it, every time,' Miss Lincoln said excitedly, her Oxford accent spear-sharp.

'I love "A Grammarian's Funeral",' I said, straying in search of further means of operating the 'clicking' mechanism.

'I can't place that just now,' Miss Lincoln said.

The beach was wild, lonely, a long stretch of surf rolling forever with the moon staying in Tauranga across the harbour on the other side, yet following us, looking down with its hint of shadowy peaks, making a path across the open sea towards Ocean Beach Road. Miss Lincoln pointed to a dark mass now sharing the horizon with the sea.

'That's Matakana Island, planted with pine trees; and next is Rabbit Island.'

She pointed to our left, behind us.

'That's the Mount.'

I had grown used to the North Islanders' reference to hills as mountains.

'And beyond the end of Ocean Beach Road, around the corner, you can see White Island, on fire with volcanic eruption.'

I looked intelligently towards where White Island would be visible.

We arrived at a small whitewashed beach cottage which I immediately likened to Haworth Parsonage. Only the gravel road and the sandhills lay between the cottage and the wintry ocean. The front of the section was an expanse of sand, where a few plants grey-leaved, stunted in growth, leaned away from the wind towards the cottage.

Once inside, Miss Lincoln showed me to a book-lined room with a big sagging bed in the middle and a wooden sandstrewn floor. It was cold, stark. The rusted window catch would not work. The casement window felt frozen with the dark massed beyond it, for the moon, having followed us home, had retreated leaving pitch dark except for the flashes of light made by the crashing breakers.

'I've already gathered pipis,' Miss Lincoln said. 'For the special meal.'

All the ingredients were there, once described faithfully by Frank Sargeson in his *Up on to the Roof and Down Again* when he and the woman he called K (Miss Lincoln) had eaten the meal here at Mount Maunganui. And as Miss Lincoln cooked our meal she quoted from Frank's description, word for word, 'Oh God, I hope not too much' as she added liquid to the rice. That paragraph from Frank's description belonged indisputably to her, and she flaunted with delight the scene where she and Frank had shared the stage.

She opened a bottle of wine. 'Keats' favourite wine,' she said. 'You'll be visiting his house in London, won't you, if you get the grant?'

I had a sense of being borne along on the wishes of others, but that was not unusual in my life. The momentum frightened me: I had no desire to travel anywhere ... but where could I live? I knew it was time to leave Esmonde Road, and there was no hope of my having a small house of my own with enough money for necessities, for if I had applied to the Literary Fund for money to spend thus, surely it would be denied. The magic enticement was 'broadening experience overseas'.

'I supppose you have all kinds of plans for overseas?'

'Well . . .' I felt ashamed of my simple desires – haunted by Wordsworth's sonnet

> Tax not the royal Saint with vain expense,
> With ill-matched aims the Architect who planned
> (Albeit labouring for a scanty band
> Of white-robed Scholars only) this immense
> And glorious work of fine intelligence!

I dreamed of seeing King's College Chapel, Cambridge. I wanted to roam the countryside of the Scholar Gypsy, and that of the Hardy novels; to see, in Shakespeare country, the 'bank whereon the wild thyme grows'; and even to walk in Kew Gardens among the lilacs! – all unfashionable dreams in a new age of *Speaking for Ourselves*. I longed also to wander in the *Euganean Hills*,

> Many a green isle needs must be
> In the deep wide sea of Misery,
> Or the mariner, worn and wan
> Never thus could voyage on
> Day and night, and night and day . . .

and to see

> The blue Mediterranean, where he lay,
> Lulled by the coil of his crystalline streams . . .

These romantic images of countryside and academic seclusion were balanced by those of 'dark satanic mills' and the squalor of the cities, for I'd heard again and again of how we in New Zealand could never imagine the squalor of cities like London, Paris, Glasgow, and when I tried to imagine being in, say, London, I furnished my images with darkness and poverty and wild-eyed medieval characters, set against tall grey stone buildings.

'I haven't really thought where I'll be,' I said.

That night for dessert we had gritty strawberry-tasting guavas from the bush growing outside the back door beside the dunny, and as this was my first taste of guavas, Miss Lincoln watched anxiously while I tasted – savoured – the new fruit, and when I declared my approval, she looked pleased, as if I had been judging her. She was sensitive also about her house and her possessions. I told her that I loved her place by the sea; there was a feeling that it lay in the middle of the sea, while the book-lined room was ideal.

'I shall read and read and read.'

I was slightly nervous, however, of Miss Lincoln – Paul – for she had announced soon after our meeting that she always 'said honestly what she thought.' Although I value honesty I am sometimes fearful of the sharpness, the hint of aggression with which it is often expressed.

'I say what I think,' Miss Lincoln repeated. Her English voice had a quelling effect. I resolved to be careful not to make myself the target of disapproval or censure, for it is usually only in such climate of conversation that people proclaim they are being 'strictly honest'.

'Have you read *The Well of Loneliness* by Radcliffe Hall?' she asked as I was going to my room. I had not read or heard of it. She said that if I wished to read it I would find it on the bookshelf, that it was one of the earliest books written about lesbianism, and that there had been a scandal over its publication.

'You know I'm a Lesbian,' she said.

'Yes. Frank said something about it, I think.' I spoke lightly, out of my depth.

I read the book that evening, in a curious turmoil of distaste and wondering as I tried to imagine women making physical love to women – I, who had never made love to anyone! The next day I believed and felt sympathy for Miss Lincoln when she explained that she'd had a lifelong passion for a schoolgirl at her former public school. She talked of Lily as if Lily were there in front of her and the passion were still alive. Tears came to her eyes.

'Lily was so beautiful.'

Lily had been her lasting, only love. Although there had been friends since who 'clicked' there had been no love as with men and women.

I decided that I liked Paul, that she was just another of the misunderstood misfits of the world. I was repelled by the idea of both male and female homosexuality yet I was learning slowly to accept the sacred differences in people although I was then ignorant of biological and hormonal facts. I knew then only that such sexual differences threatened and hurt those who loved the opposite sex.

I understood the way Paul was distressed in recounting past experiences, her longing for what had been and what had not been, and I knew that like all outcasts she would need to struggle doubly hard to survive the daily raids on her sensitivity. It occurred to me that she was almost the same age as my mother had been – two or three years younger, and here we were talking to each other as two persons. This, more than sexual confessions, occupied my thoughts during my stay, and each time we found a new topic of conversation – literature, Frank and his early life and friends, the Mount, New Zealand as it appeared to an English woman, I thought to myself, What would mother have talked about, had she and I ever been simply two persons talking? Mother, her thoughts glued to her family, so that when she might have tried to speak as a person she would find among her thoughts fragment-fibres of 'your father', 'the kiddies', 'the cows', 'the grocery order from the Self Help', 'the bill from Calder Mackays for the blankets' ... I couldn't believe that Miss Lincoln and mother would have shared historical memories and thoughts about them. When had mother time to read a book?

I could do as I wished, Paul said, during my stay. There was a bike I could ride and the sandy flat terrain was excellent for biking. Also, she wondered if I would like to meet some of her friends? There was Michael Hodgkins (the nephew of Frances Hodgkins), who lived in a small bach across the harbour but came to the beach to walk and find shells. There were also the Gilberts, Mr Gilbert, a well-known conchologist and his wife Sarah, a connoisseur of interesting people. They were a clever family, 'one of the old families', and their daughter in London knew several poets.

I was impressed.

'The only thing,' Paul said with a slight note of complaint, 'is that when I bring my interesting friends to the Mount, Sarah

Gilbert is inclined to steal them, and eventually they become *her* friends rather than mine.' At that stage of my life I could not quite imagine the importance of some of the territorial urgencies and restrictions of human friendship. How could I have forgotten so quickly all the tricks of desperation that people will use to assure and reassure themselves of their place, their p(a)lace? The desperation of people in their 'ordinary' setting was no less intense, though less visible, than among people classed as abnormal; and in both cases the desperation may be increased by the surroundings!

Here was the sandy bleak Mount Maunganui where few came in winter, where even the plants had to be bedded in sacking to help them survive; the lonely sandswept roads; the few households where the occupants waited as they wait on islands and peninsulas everywhere for news from the mainland, for interesting visitors to remind them of the continued existence of themselves and their three-sided world leased at the sea's pleasure. I could perceive now that the enticement of friends from one household to another might be something to be feared, and if the friend were lost, then the loss would be bitter.

Fortunately, the Mount's acknowledged eccentric, treasured for himself and for being the nephew of the famous painter, was shared by all. He came one day to the bach, waiting outside for us to walk with him on the beach. He was perhaps in his mid-forties; tall, dark, thin, greatly unwashed, with piercing blue eyes that looked always elsewhere. We walked on the beach, gathered shells and returned to the bach for a cup of tea, and although he did enter the sitting room, he showed his unease at being within four walls, and quickly moved outside again within sight of the surf, and once again at home on the beach, he relaxed, partly with us, partly with the sea and sky. He appeared almost to be a relic which his aunt, the famous painter, might have arranged to leave, as some painters may paint a mysterious figure within their canvas or leave an unexplained reference of colour and light that remains a source of wonder.

I met also Miss Lincoln's friends, the Gilberts. Mr Gilbert sat in a corner of the room by the fire knitting a jersey with wool that he himself had gathered, spun, and carded. Sarah, his wife, served afternoon tea of scones and cakes from a tiered fancy plate with a handle, and while Mr Gilbert spoke little, although now and again exchanging an amused glance with Miss Lincoln, ('we understand each other,' Miss Lincoln said later), Mrs Gilbert having learned of my application for a grant to travel overseas to 'broaden my experience', talked of her daughter in London who knew several well known poets, and was a close friend of one in particular. She mentioned a name. Had I read his work? Yes, I had read a poem in a Penguin anthology.

I listened with awe, a sense of failure, a pang of envy, as she explained how much her daughter was part of the literary life of London.

(And I was secretly trying to subdue my panic at the thought of the buildings, the city iself!)

Still talking of her daughter and the poet, she said securely, comfortably, 'They're very close.'

Sarah Gilbert was a woman of strength. I could see how she had 'lured' (using the word in its original sense of bait) some of Miss Lincoln's friends. Even Miss Lincoln had responded to the lure.

'She's a member of one of the *earliest* families,' she reminded me. 'Both she and her husband – they're *the* Gilberts.'

My stay with Miss Lincoln (I couldn't really say 'Paul' to her face) was made more memorable by the books I read – *Alice in Wonderland, Alice Through the Looking Glass*, the Borrower tales, the books of Beatrix Potter – none of which I had read before; and the *Complete Sermons* of Dr John Donne. At night I lay in bed reading while the waves crashed just beyond the cottage and the wind raced the sand along the dunes between us and the beach, leaving a layer of sand in the front gardens of Ocean Beach Road, in the guttering on the roof, the cracks in the walls, down the chimney, with always a small drift of sand just inside the door as a promise and reminder of invasion.

And each day in her plain white blouse and grey flannel slacks, like a refugee from an old-fashioned girls' school, Miss Lincoln knelt by her battered hedge plants, binding them with strips of sacking tied to the manuka stakes – the right dress, I thought, for plants living here by the sea; for Miss Lincoln, like Frank Sargeson,

175

had an intense dislike of 'frills and fripperies', and so even the plants were clothed to her taste. Not being able to give up my lifelong fascination with clothes which I longed for but never had, yet might some day acquire even if it were by the ultimate magic of unfolding layer upon layer of silk from a small brown hazelnut, I usually felt slightly ashamed when Frank or Miss Lincoln began their tirade against what they called 'feminine fripperies'. They reminded me of my father and his, 'What do you want clothes for? You've got a perfectly good school uniform.'

In spite of their plain dress, however, the Mount Maunganui, the *Haworth Parsonage* hedge plants wore proudly a special, glittering ribbon of salt and rainbow light borrowed from the ocean.

A few days before I was to return to Auckland, the telegram came from Frank.

'Privately informed. Three hundred pounds granted. Congratulations.'

So my journey away from New Zealand was to be a reality. I had so little notion of the value of money that I could not judge whether three hundred pounds which to me seemed like a fortune, was much or little, or how it would provide me with fare and expenses, and for how long.

Miss Lincoln shared my excitement at the news. The evening before I left, we celebrated as we had done on the first night, with pipis and rice ('Oh my God I hope not too much!') and the red wine of Keats. And as I was packing my small suitcase, Miss Lincoln brought in a carefully folded pair of grey flannel slacks.

'They will fit you,' she said. 'Take them, for your journey.'

I tried them on. They fitted. I could not tell her that I disliked wearing slacks, that I thought these were ugly with baggy legs, and the grey flannel reminded me too much of our old Junior High uniform.

The next day I travelled again through the wilderness of bush-enclosed railway track to Auckland and its wet wintry world and upper-sky light, and as I now had an almost visible 'future', my life took on a new excitement as Frank and I waited for the official announcement of the grant, and the cheque for three hundred pounds.

26
Advice to the Traveller

I received official notification of my grant but before the cheque was sent the Advisory Committee requested that I be interviewed by one of its members, Miss Louden, a former school headmistress living in Auckland. This was to be the beginning, after my known length of stay in hospital, of a number of investigations of my sanity by people who would try to find out for themselves whether I was incurably ill as the medical diagnosis would imply, or whether (as was later proved during my time in London) there had been an awful mistake even in my first admission to hospital, and from then a continued misinterpretation of my plight. The general opinion of the literary world then is confirmed by the reference in *The New Zealand Encyclopedia* to my 'tragic disordered power' and 'unstable personality', an opinion repeated many times by people unknown to me.

Frank, as usual, tried to cheer me when I learned of the interview.

'It'll be nothing,' he said. 'Just put on the schoolgirl act, being agreeable and polite in front of the headmistress.'

He assured me that Miss Louden was a pleasant, sensible, intelligent person who would realize that, whatever she thought of my 'history', the best move for me was to get away from New Zealand.

A few days later I travelled on the bus to Remuera for my interview with Miss Louden where, in between drinking tea and eating scones and cakes from yet another fancily tiered plate, I tried to impress with my 'normality', presenting myself as a happy healthy woman. Miss Louden, like most retired women teachers I had heard of, lived in a house packed with furniture and books in rooms with carpets patterned rose and dark red, like cinema carpets; while she herself had the air of being packed with Culture. I spoke in what I hoped was a fearless manner about my trip overseas, whereupon she began to talk of my schooldays and in reply to her questions on topics closed centuries ago – sport, prefects, the Sixth Form – I listed my long-past activities – captain of the B basketball team, Physical Training Shield, House Captain, Proxime Accessit to Dux . . . and so on, playing her chosen game of yesterdays.

It was a pleasant if perspiry afternoon; and I knew that I had succeeded when Frank, through the eternally pruned, fertilized, growing and fruiting literary grapevine of which he appeared to be the Auckland keeper, heard that Miss Louden had judged me to be a 'normal, happy, healthy *girl*.'

The cheque arrived. I gazed unbelievingly at it. I showed it to Frank.

'What shall I do with it?' I asked. I had never had a bank account, for, like so many other facilities, bank accounts were thought to be for 'other people'. In our family, only Myrtle had ever had a bank account, a Post Office Savings Book, with three and sixpence entered one week and two and sixpence withdrawn the next, leaving the magic shilling which was said to keep the account 'open'. When Myrtle died, the shilling and a few pence were returned, and the face of the page stamped *Cancelled, Withdrawn*.

That afternoon, instead of taking his usual rest, Frank went with me and the cheque to the Bank of New South Wales where he introduced me to the manager. I was a highly recommended client, he said, praising me as a writer.

My next move was to pay seventy-eight pounds for a berth in a six-berth cabin in the *Ruahine* sailing from Wellington to Southampton at the end of July. I then applied for a passport and arranged for a primary vaccination for smallpox. I was on my way overseas!

The advice poured in, the first and most valuable from Jess Whitworth who had twice travelled to Europe on the savings from her pension and who knew a place in London where I might be able to stay. I visited her and her husband, Ernest, at Northcote and spent the afternoon listening to her disarming accounts of her travels. She had made her first journey when she was seventy, sailing alone while Ernest, who was not interested in physical travel, stayed at home with the stereo record player he had built, and listened to his collection of Schubert and Mozart. Anyone who knew Jess will say that she was a remarkable woman. She had a talented family from her first marriage with Oliver Duff. She had written a vivid account of her childhood as the daughter of a pubkeeper in Central Otago, and her girlhood in Dunedin, in her book *Otago Interval* which even then was out of print and so unknown to many. Jess had been a music teacher and shared her love of music with her second husband. She was eager, wise, literate, adventurous, and soft-hearted, while Ernest, some years younger, was everlastingly devoted to her.

It was a curious chance that six months after mother's death I was befriended by two women of her generation who perhaps in their late childhood were alike in their fondness for the arts and their possession of an extra store of imagination, yet whose lives were notable for their differences, and for what remained in each in the long struggle for survival. Jess, too, had had the time of many children and many nappies in a household without too much money. Paula or Paul Lincoln had broken away from her family; mother's marriage had estranged her from her disapproving family. Listening to Jess and her tales of travel, I couldn't help thinking of the lifetime of words that mother never spoke: I saw them marching in single or double file (as words do) to the tip of her tongue, then being turned away because the time was not right or there was no-one to receive them, and even her hastily written poems and letters to the editor and prayers to God could not have released all the furious prisoners crowded in the anterooms of her thoughts. If only she had been able to *speak for herself!*

Jess was full of advice: I should buy one or two metal dishes for cooking, and a small metal cooker to use with solid methylated spirits, so that if I had to stay in a hotel I could save money by making my own tea, boiling eggs, and so on. There was a woman who kept a boardinghouse in Clapham Common, with a row of

179

garden rooms at the back of the house, Jess explained, and there were always rooms vacant for seventeen shillings a week. For my first few nights in London, she recommended that I stay in the Hostel of the *Society of Friends* in Euston Square, and that I write to them at once, booking my room. As she travelled only in the European summer, with her cooking utensils, two dresses and a petticoat also worn as a nightdress, two or three pairs of pants, that is, with as little luggage as possible, she wasn't able to advise on winter clothes. She suggested a money belt.

'A money belt?'

'You put your money in it and fasten it around your waist; or make a small bag and tie it around your neck, dropping it down your bosom.'

'Oh.'

Jess always visited Salzburg, staying in a pension 'around the corner from Mozart's birthplace.' Before I left her home that afternoon, she sat at her old walnut-gold piano, and played two early pieces by Mozart.

She laughed. 'Early! He composed these when he was six!'

Next, Frank's friends, returned from Spain, also gave advice.

'If you want to make your money last,' they said, 'Ibiza is the place.'

'Ibiza?'

'It's spelt with a "z" but you say it the Spanish way, "th".'

'Oh.'

'You can live on the island of Ibiza for three or four pounds a month.'

Frank reminded me that Greville now lived at Tossa, with a flat in Barcelona, and he would write to her, and they'd meet me at Barcelona and see me on to the boat at Ibiza.

'I suppose Ibiza would be the place to stay, then, as I shan't have much money.'

'See, here it is on the map, just below Majorca and Minorca. Majorca where *Robert Graves* lives.'

'Robert Graves!'

We'd been reading his prose and poetry. Frank's friends told how friends of theirs had visited Majorca and called on Robert Graves! They met Freya Stark, too.

'Freya Stark?'

'The travel writer.'

'Oh.'

Everyone had tales of travel! Everyone talked of what to do, where to go, what to expect, while I listened proud, pleased, and frightened. One evening Una Platts arrived with hilarious stories of sailing through the Suez canal to London. The Suez Canal. The white slave traffic! Una wore a pleated skirt which she identified as 'terylene'.

'It's new,' she said. 'You never have to iron it. The pleats are *permanent.*'

(Oh for a permanently pleated skirt!)

The questions of clothes for the journey had begun to occupy me. My images of all factors in the northern hemisphere, including weather (the descriptions gleaned from the Anglo-Saxon 'Wanderer' and 'Seafarer'), were extreme, stark, and terrifying, and I saw my clothes as at least a first protection against the northern danger.

'All you need,' Frank said (beginning his counsel exactly as my father would have done) 'is Paul's slacks and a blouse. Plus the cardigan you knitted.' During the recent weeks of waiting, like a woman expecting a child, I had begun to knit, making an outsize grey pullover for Frank and for myself a large fawn cardigan with a hood, the fawn chosen because I was not brave enough to chose a *real* colour. Lately I had been studying the brochures from the shipping company, with the impressive photos of women wearing glittering evening clothes and fashionable sunsuits, with one special photo of a woman in a slinky backless dress getting ready for dinner while a handsome man in a flared jacket fixed her zip; they were laughing, she glancing at him in a romantic way, óver her shoulder. Shipboard life was portrayed as a whirlwind of sexual ecstasy with meeting eyes and hands and the promise of meeting bodies with all the passengers handsome and beautiful and dressed in the highest fashion and during the day so constantly active with games, walks, dining at tables laden with roast turkey, lobsters, trifle, champagne, dancing the moonlight hours away, that one might have wondered if there were enough energy left for the remaining night's activities. I could scarcely believe that I was to be among these passengers, even perhaps wearing a backless evening dress while someone, laughing, fixed my zip.

My fantasies perished as soon as they were born. I was to live the Spartan life. Clothes did not matter.

Yet, seeing my three hundred pounds fast diminishing, I collected a suitcase of my fairly new clothes, and taking the ferry to town, sitting among all the morning shoppers in their white gloves and hats, for everyone in those days 'dressed' to go to town, I hawked my clothes in the second-hand shops where I quickly found that my pleas of 'but they're almost brand new' brought the same response, 'They're worth almost nothing.' I could feel the growing misery and panic of being face to face with the 'real' world where nobody cared, where people were hard-faced, mercenary – city people; and I couldn't even console myself by thinking, It doesn't matter, because it did matter, I had to supplement my money. I wanted to give my radiogram and records to Frank, but he insisted that I sell it; yet one more hard-faced shopkeeper gave me ten pounds, and I gave the records to my sister. Then, miraculously, an 'anonymous donor' whom I guessed correctly to be Charles Brasch, sent fifty pounds to Frank 'for Janet to buy some clothes for her journey.' Surprisingly, I was now the Spartan, insisting that fifty pounds was too precious to waste on 'mere clothes'. All the same, I again took the ferry to Auckland where I hoped to sell my new *Mademoiselle Modes* olive-green coat. Surely I thought, remembering the struggle to save the ten pounds, and the pleasure of buying the coat, surely it is worth something.

'Two shillings, no more,' the shop assistant said.

I decided to keep it rather than see it thrown among a heap of shiny baggy cast-off clothes in the dingy sweat-and-mothball-smelling shop.

Then, wanting to make my own plans for my journey, I bought an old *Fodor's Guide to Europe* which I took back to the hut without showing it to Frank who might have thought me extravagant to buy it. As I read the guide I found myself becoming more dazed, confused, excited, and alarmed. Was travelling overseas really like this? The guide was packed with information all presented as important, much of it in lists of what to buy and where to buy it, details of the best bargains in leather, silk, woollen goods, furs, china, jewellery, with the names of the shops, the cities, the countries where the goods were held, the assumption being that every traveller was a merchant in search of prized bargains. The guide also contained lists of sights to see – museums, galleries, cathedrals; tours to take; clothes to pack for the tours; and finally, *Common Words and Phrases in many Languages* (which I quickly dealt with by tearing out the pages and pasting them on a cardboard folder to consult during my journey).

I studied the advice on clothing. The traveller to wintry Europe, the books stressed, should wear a heavy coat with a warm removable lining that would double as a dressing-gown.

I promptly bought four yards of cheap molleton cloth, striped blue-grey, and tried without success to sew a coat lining: the result bunched, and would not 'hang' and parts of it drooped beneath my coat. I also bought from the Army Surplus store a green canvas haversack, an army cooking pan with a folding handle, and three small green canvas bags like a child's marble-bags, for use as money-bags. Frank had said that a haversack was better than a suitcase. His friends had reminded me that if you travelled by sea you always took a *cabin trunk*. How deprived was I, I wondered, not having a cabin trunk?

My visits to my sister's at Northcote also resulted in gleanings of advice. When my sister's English friend heard that I was planning to stay at Clapham Common, she stared at me in horror.

'Clapham? Surely not! I wouldn't recommend it. It's terribly *urban*, so *urban*,' with her feelings centred on the word *urban*. I wondered if perhaps I had mistaken the meaning of urban, if it now meant more than 'of the city'.

'What do you mean, urban?'

'You know, *urban*. Factories and so on.'

From that moment I had my image of where I would be staying in London. I saw a street without people, with a succession of factories, huge buildings like aerodromes, each with a small grey door opening on to the street. My garden room would be set between two factories, down a narrow alley with another small door leading to a square of concrete, with no sign of a real garden, the name having been given only in a burst of wishful dreaming. I was completely alone in the street of factories, where the machines worked noisily day and night without the attendance of people. I thought of Jess Whitworth's description of her 'tackling' a big city, how she first found her place to stay, then left her luggage and set out to 'find her bearings', noting the names and streets and the different shops where she would buy her provisions, then after her preliminary exploration, returning home to 'gather steam' (many of her metaphors were nautical) for venturing further afield. I tried to picture myself walking miles and miles with no sign of people or shops, then returning along that narrow alley to my 'Garden Room'. During those weeks before my journey, my mind swarmed with so many foreboding images of the northern hemisphere that I wonder, in retrospect, if I was as clear-headed as I thought myself to be, and I can partly explain when I remember that I was again surrounded by people who were planning my future.

I was again living the submissive, passive role which in hospital had been forced upon me but which my shy nature had accommodated with ease: at its best it is the role of the queen bee surrounded by her attendants; at its worst it is that of the victim without power or possession; and in both cases there is no ownership of one's self, for all have a stake in the planned future.

My passport arrived. I had my ticket (with return travel guaranteed by the anonymous donor of the fifty pounds for clothes), and I'd booked my sleeping berth on the night express to Wellington.

Then I became ill, very ill with the effect of the smallpox vaccination. I felt as if I were dying. I lay only half-conscious in the hut while Frank spoon-fed me with *Farex* mixed with milk, the kind of food given to babies and kittens separated early from their mother. And just when I was recovering from the vaccination I was stricken with the influenza, called the '1918 'flu' that spread over Auckland that year. My recovery was slow as I was now dreading the prospect of travelling anywhere. Frank, ever kind and patient, tried to cheer me as one would cheer a sick child, bringing items to distract and please – a glass globe enclosing a snowstorm, a Japanese paper flower that opened in water. He hung Chinese wind chimes at the open door of the hut where they played a tinkling tune as the breeze passed through the window and out into the space of garden by the pawpaw tree.

Neither Frank nor I could disguise our feeling of gloom as if it were the end of a century or the extinction of a race that had survived over millions of years; there was an exaggeration of time as if like a creature deprived of its shell, it quivered, being touched or even glanced at; it was like the silkworm cut away from its mass of silk.

Our friends Karl and Kay had gone from Auckland. We missed them greatly and looked forward eagerly to their letters from Armidale. Maurice Duggan was despondent, not working. Frank took me one day to see Maurice and Barbara and the custard apple tree and we sat in a large airy room listening to Victoria Los Angeles; and copies of *The Paris Review* lay on a small table. *The Paris Review*. I looked at Maurice (described by Frank as 'the suffering romantic') and Barbara and it seemed to me that they were clever and literary and their subtle colours would have delighted the art lecturer at Training College. I was still overendowed with the capacity to gape with wonder, to marvel at everything and everyone, and the world.

Fragments of tasks remained: Albion Wright of the Pegasus Press disliking my title, *Talk of Treasure*, suggested I choose another. I thought of *Within Sound of the Sea* but he said No, there had recently been a book, *Within Sound of the Bell* (by a school teacher). What about *When Owls Do Cry*? I said. No, *Owls Do Cry*, he said.

In the evenings now I sat listening to the latest topic of conversation. 'Janet is going to Ibiza to live until her money runs out ...' 'Janet plans to go to London first, then take the train south ... she will probably stay overnight in Paris ... then to Barcelona ... then take the boat to the Balearic Islands ... Janet is ... Janet will be ... Janet has ...'

Beneath my gloom was a rising sense of adventure. I knew that Frank's gloom concealed a feeling of relief that he would be free

185

to continue more peacefully with his writing. I could not even remember how it had been decided that I would leave the country; I knew only that there was no way back, that if my path did lead back there would be no second chance for my survival, that it was best for me to escape from a country where, since my student days, a difference which was only myself, and even my ambition to write, had been looked on as evidence of abnormality.

But – oh, I was daunted by the length and unfamiliarity of the path forward, the sea journey across the immense Pacific, across the English Channel, the night in Paris, travelling through France, Spain, across the Mediterranean! Why? I was sustained then, as ever, by the prospect of seeing through 'Shelley's eyes' the landscape and

> The blue Mediterranean, where he lay,
> Lulled by the coil of his crystalline streams.

27
The Traveller

Like a mythical character about to embark on a long voyage, I had first to undergo a test, a refining process supervised by my family and lasting four days until my ship sailed. I was to stay with Aunty Polly and Uncle Vere in Petone while my father who usually travelled north at this time of year for Rugby matches, would also be in Wellington at Aunty Polly's. Mother's two sisters, Elsie and Joy, hoped to see me in Wellington. After a long trainsick journey from Auckland I dreaded the polishing process that is a result of the natural friction within families.

At Petone Aunty Polly showed me to my bed, a low canvas camp stretcher propped just inside the door of the sitting room, low enough to receive the icy blast from beneath the back door.

'Your father, of course, will have the bed in the spare room.'

'Oh, of course.'

She looked sternly at me. 'I can't understand why you're leaving your father to go all that way overseas. Your mother has just died, and your place is at home looking after your father.'

I had no answer to that. We were meeting Dad the next morning at the ferry wharf.

Then Aunty Polly turned her attention to my clothes. (Aunty Polly the clever dressmaker who even now had her small workroom spread with 'difficult' sewing – men's coats, trousers, suits and women's dresses with fancy sleeves and bodices.)

'What on earth are you wearing that horrible cardigan for? It's far too big and it's an awful colour, it's just no colour at all. You look like a piece of earth or something, wearing it. And you can see your whole shape through your skirt!'

'I knitted this cardigan,' I said proudly. 'And the colour goes with everything.'

'It's drab.'

Once Aunty Polly had made her criticism she became kinder. 'So you've had the 'flu. Well you don't want to catch cold.'

That evening when Uncle Vere, tall, gentle with cowlike brown eyes, came home from the Motor Works Aunty Polly submitted him, in his turn, to her judgement of his appearance, 'Just look at your scarf, it shouldn't be that way. What have you done to your coat, the way it hangs?'

Dressmaker to the world! Like an artist who is constantly framing the view, isolating and freezing objects in order to transform them with imagination.

When Uncle Vere had been transformed to Aunty Polly's liking, there was ordinary conversation once again, even kindness and laughter.

I went to bed early, huddling into the one blanket while the bitter Wellington wind swept under the door and between the canvas and the frame of my sagging bed.

Next morning Aunty Polly drove me in her frog-green car to meet Dad at the ferry, and when I saw him coming down the gangway with his greying hair even greyer in the wintry light of sky and sea, and his forlorn look stemming from an inner dishevelment of grief (though he was outwardly smart with his polished shoes and spic and span best suit), I burst into tears and went towards him. I hadn't seen him since mother's death. His lip, pouting in infant shape, trembled, and we embraced each other and cried. Dad, unlike Aunty Polly, was proud of my grant and my journey overseas, and his sense of pride, when aroused, could always quell other more painful feelings.

'So you're going home,' he said.

I was startled. I had never heard him call the northern hemisphere *home*; he had usually laughed at people who still talked of the United Kingdom as *Home*; I had heard him say scornfully, 'Home, my foot. Here's home right here. Or I'll go hopping sideways to Puketeraki.'

During my stay I heard him repeat several times, 'Janet's going home, you know.' I found myself acquiring a prestige which almost covered my identity as the 'mad niece'. I was now the 'niece who is going overseas, *home*.'

I realized suddenly that my father's use of the word 'home' was in deference to Aunty Polly and Uncle Vere and the other relations, for it was *their* language which he with an intuitive courtesy or a dislike of appearing different, had adopted. He also used his knife and fork in a different way, Aunty Polly's way. And he didn't fart once. Aunty Polly and Uncle Vere, as I have said, were thought of as being 'in society', a nebulous fluctuating area bordered by a few mayors and councillors and other acknowledged 'important' people. 'He's someone, you know,' Aunty Polly used to say. I never heard her say of a person, 'He's no-one,' but she did imply that not everybody was somebody.

Mother's sisters Elsie and Joy took me to morning tea at Kirkcaldies. They too were critical of my clothes and of the fact that I had not 'met my fate', that is, married, but their kind of criticism was without sharpness or bitterness. They were beautiful women who melted into laughter as they reminisced about Kirkcaldies as it had been in their youth. They were gentle, kindly, concerned, Aunty Joy's brown eyes showing flashes of apprehension and startle like the look in a wild creature's eyes and because I did not know her well, I could not guess at the origin of that glance.

Both, insisting that I would need a heavier coat for the northern winter, went 'halves' in buying me a warm brown coat.

'Now you look smarter,' they said.

And even Aunty Polly approved of my new coat.

'At least it covers up that awful jacket.'

I forgave her; it is a responsibility, being dressmaker to the world.

The *Ruahine* came into port. It was the evening of my departure. Aunty Polly, Uncle Vere and Dad saw me on to the ship, helped me find the six-berth cabin down several layers from the main deck, then, almost as if they were afraid to be captured, as if the ship were a prison, they went ashore on to the wharf.

'We won't be staying to see her go out.'

Dad spoke proudly of the ship as he used to speak of the train-engine, calling it 'she' and 'her'. He used to call the rivers 'she' also, looking at them with a weatherwise eye and warning, 'She's coming down dirty . . .'

I stood on deck among a crowd of passengers, all throwing streamers that were caught by the watchers on the wharf, for in those days travelling by ship was a momentous occasion. There was a brass band playing old tunes, Maori songs, and a few military marches. I stayed on deck to catch one more glimpse of Aunty Polly, looking frailly neat in her blue coat, Uncle Vere, tall beside her, and Dad, huddled against the wind, in the half-shelter of the wharf shed, then with a final wave, and clutching the five-pound note that Aunty Polly had pressed into my hand with a whispered 'Something from Uncle Vere and myself', I went towards the stairs, just as the band was playing *Now is the Hour*, and the music reached down like a long spoon inside me and stirred, and stirred.

I came to my six-berth cabin, with my lower berth by the door. Accepting the advice of those who knew better than I, I had brought with me a small oval bottle of lavender smelling salts and a small tin of water biscuits and a tube of *Kwells* seasick preventative. I put these in a locker drawer; rather disdainfully, for I knew I would not need them. I felt the throbbing of the engines and the slow movement of the ship as it sailed out of Wellington Harbour.

'It's good,' I thought, all fears of seasickness vanishing. 'My first ocean voyage and it's running smoothly.'

I went up on deck. It was too soon for the appearance of the passengers dancing and wearing evening dress, but somewhere there was music playing, and the sound of talking and laughter.

The lights of Wellington now shone in the distance. I leaned over the deck-rail and I felt like weeping with fear and delight. Then suddenly the motion of the ship changed to a steeper rise and fall and rolling from side to side: we were on the open sea. My voyage had begun.